CULTURE-PROTESTANTISM

AMERICAN ACADEMY OF RELIGION
STUDIES IN RELIGION SERIES

edited by
Stephen Crites

Number 15
CULTURE-PROTESTANTISM:
German Liberal Theology at the Turn of the Twentieth Century

by
George Rupp

SCHOLARS PRESS
Missoula, Montana

CULTURE-PROTESTANTISM:
German Liberal Theology at the Turn of the Twentieth Century

by
George Rupp

Published by
SCHOLARS PRESS
for
The American Academy of Religion

Distributed by

SCHOLARS PRESS
Missoula, Montana 59806

CULTURE-PROTESTANTISM:
German Liberal Theology at the Turn of the Twentieth Century

by
George Rupp

Library of Congress Cataloging in Publication Data
Rupp, George.
   Culture-protestantism : German liberal theology at
the turn of the twentieth century.

   (American Academy of Religion studies in religion
series ; no. 15 ISSN 0084-6287)
   Includes bibliographical references.
   1. Theology, Protestant—Germany—History. 2.
Christianity and culture—History. 3. Liberalism
(Religion)—Germany—History. I. Title. II. Series:
American Academy of Religion. AAR studies in
religion ; no. 15.
BT30.G3R86   230'.0943   77-13763
ISBN 0-89130-197-6

Printed in the United States of America
1 2 3 4 5

For my parents

Erika Braunöhler Rupp
and
Gustav Wilhelm Rupp

ACKNOWLEDGMENTS

This study is gratefully dedicated to my parents. Among their innumerable gifts to me are two which figure prominently in this essay: an interest in religious questions and an early exposure to the German language.

Along with my gratitude to my parents, I want to express my appreciation to my wife Nancy and to our children Kathy and Stephanie for their willingness and even eagerness to undergo the challenge of immersion in German language and culture.

I am also grateful to Harvard University, its Divinity School, and the Association of Theological Schools for support during the spring of 1976 when this study was researched and written.

For careful reading of the essay in typescript and perceptive suggestions for revision, I want to thank the following colleagues and friends: Walter F. Bense of the University of Wisconsin—Oshkosh; Van A. Harvey of Stanford University; and Wayne Proudfoot of Columbia University. And to Stephen D. Crites, the editor of the *AAR Studies in Religion,* I want to express my appreciation for detailed feedback during the decision-making process, for steady support through a period of delays, and for extremely helpful suggestions for revision.

Finally, I want to thank Linda Kettner of the Theology Department at Harvard Divinity School for her expert preparation of the typescript.

TABLE OF CONTENTS

1   Culture-Protestantism

For at least two generations, theologically interested approaches to the religious situation at the turn of the twentieth century have been so under the influence of polemic that only a very partial and often unbalanced portrayal has resulted. Especially in the case of Germany, the religious thought of this period has almost unavoidably been viewed through the double prism of the catastrophe of World War I and the emergence of dialectical theology or Neo-orthodoxy. This prism attracts attention to a significant range of issues. But analysis and appraisal of the various positions on the resulting spectrum are intimately involved with attitudes toward Neo-orthodoxy itself. This influence of Neo-orthodoxy is epitomized in the association of the term "Culture-Protestantism" with the thought of the several theological generations preceding World War I. Accordingly, consideration of the name itself and of the opposed evaluations that it conveys may serve to indicate characterizations of the period that continue to be influential even when their initial polemical intentions are no longer shared.

1.1   "Culture-Protestantism": Ambiguities in the Term

The term "Culture-Protestantism" suffers from the ambiguities characteristic of names that serve both descriptive and polemical purposes. The term is typically used as a pejorative designation. As such, it expresses the judgment that a theological position or movement acquiesces to or passively reflects the cultural ethos of its time. But the name may also be construed neutrally or even positively. An influential illustration of this orientation is the analysis of Emanuel Hirsch. After discussing Hegel and Schleiermacher as thinkers who stress the need for the Christian tradition to relate to all of modern life, Hirsch notes that the term "Culture-Protestantism" is often used in this connection:

> For this over-all stance the name "Culture-Protestantism" has been coined. Despite the fact that it is often used polemically and dragged through the mud by undiscriminating minds, this label perhaps still expresses more clearly than anything else the relationship of the Neo-Protestant idea of the church to the Enlightenment. But it must not be overlooked that a deep Christian earnestness prevails in the initiators of this perspective. Not the secularization of what is Christian but the guiding back [Heimführung] of the worldly to its religious, its Christian, ground is the final core of this thought.[1]

In this analysis, Culture-Protestantism is, then, an expression of the Christian ethical imperative to inform and shape the whole of life so that it realizes the ultimately religious significance which is its ground and end.

9

In H. Richard Niebuhr's *Christ and Culture,* the two verdicts about Culture-Protestantism meet: appreciative description is combined with systematic criticism. Hence the book offers a microcosm of the multiple meanings that the term continues to convey. And because it accurately reflects prevailing usage, it at the same time reinforces the predominance of the pejorative meaning. The significance of this reinforcing role has been considerable. *Christ and Culture* has, of course, been especially influential in American theology. That its impact has not been confined to America is, however, evident from the frequent references to it in European theological literature and from such incidental facts as the appearance in the third edition of *Religion in Geschichte und Gegenwart* of an article by D. G. Harbsmeier entitled "Kultur und Christentum, grundsätzlich"—an article which is devoted almost exclusively to an exposition of and commentary on Neibuhr's book.

In *Christ and Culture* Niebuhr appropriates the name "Culture-Protestantism" as an alternative designation for one of the five types he elaborates in his discussion of the relations between Christian faith and its varying cultural contexts. It is the second of the types, the one that he more usually terms "The Christ of Culture":

> In modern history this type is well-known, since for generations it has been dominant in a large section of Protestantism. Inadequately defined by the use of such terms as "liberal" and "liberalism," it is more aptly named Culture-Protestantism; but appearances of this type have not been confined to the modern world nor to the churches of the Reformation.[2]

As this quotation indicates, Niebuhr generalizes the type to include all interpretations that affirm cultural ideals and human institutions as continuous with the transcendent reality to which Christianity testifies. His examples range from Paul's Judaizing opponents and the Gnostics over Abelard, Locke, Kant, and Schleiermacher to "the whole period" of the nineteenth century from Hegel on as "the time of cultural Protestantism." Ritschl is considered in some detail; but also mentioned are such turn-of-the-century figures as Harnack, Rauschenbusch, and Shailer Mathews. Niebuhr works at presenting a balanced view of this tendency in Christian thought. He criticizes the attempt so to accomodate Christianity to the canons of culture that every offense is removed. But he also notes that criticisms of Culture-Protestantism not infrequently themselves illustrate the type—with the exception that the accommodation is to a past culture. Indeed, he claims that "as a perennial movement the acculturation of Christ is both inevitable and profoundly significant in the extension of his reign."[3]

Yet this serious effort to present a balanced portrayal of Culture-Protestantism is in the end frustrated because of the contrast that Niebuhr draws between this pattern and the fifth and final type, Christ the Transformer of Culture. In assigning all "conversionist" tendencies to this fifth type,

Niebuhr in effect programatically confines the Christ of Culture motif to a legitimation of the cultural *status quo*. So to formulate the issue is no doubt illuminating as a specification of systematic alternatives. But Niebuhr's identification of the nineteenth century as the period of Culture-Protestantism is also a matter of historical judgment that reflects the common view during the time when Neo-orthodoxy represented the prevailing theological mood. This judgment, which Niebuhr conveys in the course of his systematic analysis, is much more transparently polemical in the pronouncements of Karl Barth.

1.2   Karl Barth on the End of Nineteenth-Century Theology

Barth repeatedly emphasized his shock and dismay over the virtually unanimous support of his theology teachers for German military operations at the outset of World War I. Crucial for his own theological orientation was, Barth reports, the appearance in August 1914 of a manifesto that declared the support of academic and cultural leaders for the war. In a 1957 survey lecture on protestant theology in the nineteenth century, Barth observes that this day constitutes the end of that era for him:

> For me personally a day in the beginning of August in that year [1914] has impressed itself as the *dies ater*. It is the day on which 93 German intellectuals published a profession of support for the war policy of Kaiser Wilhelm II. Included among the signers I was shocked to have to see the names of pretty much all my teachers-theologians whom I had until then loyally honored. Having been estranged from their ethos, I observed that I would also no longer be able to follow their ethics and dogmatics, their exegesis and historical interpretation. For me in any case the theology of the nineteenth century had no future any more.[4]

The statement to which Barth refers is a travesty. Entitled "Appeal to the World of Culture," it is a litany of six "It is not true" assertions: Germany is not at fault for the war and did not violate the neutrality of Belgium; German troops did not infringe on the rights of civilians, were not brutal, did not violate international law; finally, so-called German militarism is not at odds with its great cultural traditions.[5] The reliance of the statement on unsubstantiated assertions and self-serving rhetoric is sufficiently blatant that it is dismaying to see scientists like Max Planck and Wilhelm Röntgen, literary and artistic figures like Max Liebermann and Gerhard Hauptmann, and humanists like Karl Lamprecht and Rudolf Eucken among the signers. And it is even more distressing to note that twelve of the 93 names are those of theologians. Even allowing for poetic license, the signers do not constitute "pretty much all" of Barth's teachers. But four of the twelve are major figures: Adolf von Harnack, Wilhelm Herrmann, Adolf von Schlatter, and Reinhold Seeberg. Insofar as Harnack and Herrmann may be taken to represent theological liberalism and Schlatter and Seeberg conservatism, the four together do, moreover, suggest central strains in the pre-war German theology that Barth declares ended with the issuing of this statement.

For Barth the ending of the era did not, however, mean uniform opposition to the various strains in nineteenth-century theology. In the preface to the second edition to *The Epistle to the Romans*, Schlatter is, for example, still mentioned appreciatively in spite of his signing of the statement supporting German actions in 1914.[6] Although conservative as well as liberal theologians supported the war effort (as did virtually everyone else within Germany during at least the first months of the fighting), Barth focuses his opposition on the liberals because he sees their self-conscious effort to relate to current cultural trends as the root of the aimlessness that can support whatever social cause offers itself. *The Epistle to the Romans* of course registers this contention in imposing and programmatic style. But Barth also personalizes the issue very pointedly in his lectures and essays just after the war. Two examples are especially striking.

The first is a pair of much-discussed and repeatedly published essays that appeared in 1919. In the essays Barth compares Friedrich Naumann and Christoph Blumhardt, both of whom died in that year. At the time of his death, Naumann was the leader of the German Democratic Party in the Reichstag. He had begun his professional life as a pastor in a mining village and then as a community worker in Frankfurt, but he had left the ministry under pressure from conservative church officials and had instead become a full-time politician. His career centered on recurrent attempts to bridge the divides between liberals and socialists. It also included support for at least some of Germany's imperial pretensions and the signing of the August 1914 appeal of 93 cultural leaders. Barth portrays Naumann so as to maximize the contrast to Blumhardt, who lived and worked as a pastor in Bad Boll, the retreat center begun by his father—a ministry he continued even after he was deprived of his clerical status for joining the Social Democratic Party and being elected to the Württemberg Landtag. The thrust of the contrast Barth draws is between Naumann as an individual committed to worldly institutions and causes (including Christianity) and Blumhardt as one who lived out of a powerful and effective hope in God's ultimate victory even on earth.

Barth insists that neutrality, that an attempt to do justice to both positions, is impossible. Rather both can be honored only if they are taken seriously enough to say Yes to one and No to the other. Barth's own verdict is as unambiguously positive over Blumhardt as it is scathingly negative over Naumann. Blumhardt represents the "victory of the future over the past." In contrast, Naumann embodies the aspirations of the pre-war era that have been irredeemably and rightly destroyed:

> If anything has been condemned as false, abolished, and annihilated through the present world catastrophe, then it is the religious and political thought-world of Friedrich Naumann. One does not go unpunished so close to the truth—and yet past it. His figure is the embodiment of the tragic greatness, guilt, and shame not only of his people but of our whole age.[7]

A second instance of personalized critique of theological liberalism is less vehement and less direct but equally uncompromising. This attack occurs in the process of defending dialectical theology through a series of exchanges with Harnack during 1923 in the journal *Die Christliche Welt*. In November of 1922 Barth had published his programmatic lecture/essay "The Word of God as the Task of Theology." Without directly naming Barth, Harnack wrote "Fifteen Questions for the Despisers of Intellectually Defensible Theology among the Theologians" for the January 1923 issue. Barth responded with "Sixteen Answers . . ." in the February issue. There followed another exchange and then a concluding postscript from Harnack in May of 1923. This series of exchanges is fascinating because it anticipates virtually all the issues that emerge between Neo-orthodoxy and its opponents in the following decades. Barth insists on the absolute or simple or unqualified (schlechthinniger) contrast between God and the world, on the centrality of the risen Christ rather than the historical Jesus, on the unassailable primacy of divine revelation over human experience, on the autonomy of theology as fidelity to the word of the Lord. Harnack worries about the threat of otherworldliness, the repudiation of all relative standards of value, the identification of theology and preaching.

In his contribution to the exchange, Barth in effect declares the theology that Harnack represents to be as deservedly dead as the thought-world of Naumann. And to be sure that the connections are not overlooked, he refers explicitly to the role of such theology in glorifying battle experiences and justifying war. Harnack enquires whether and how "experience of God" and the "awakening of faith" by God are related.[8] Barth responds that they are "as different as earth is from heaven."[9] Harnack asks how there is any protection against atheism and barbarism if the divine is absolutely different from "the development of culture and its discernment and morality."[10] Barth answers acidly:

> The assertions about God that derive "from the development of culture and its discernment and morality" (for example, the assertions of the war theologians of all countries) may have their meaning and value as the expression of special "experiences of God" (for example, war experiences) along with those of primitive peoples, who do not yet recognize such high values. As "preaching of the Gospel" . . . *these* assertions in any case do *not* merit consideration.[11]

The programmatic if often implicit assault on the entire pre-war era of liberal theology and piety that *The Epistle to the Romans* launches is, then, also conducted explicitly and personally in Barth's characterization of Naumann and in his responses to Harnack. The target of attack is designated graphically in his reference to Naumann's "religious glorification of nature and modern culture":

> *Why not?* God speaks everywhere. But imperceptibly it happened that for him the existing as such—the state and the Hohenzollern dynasty and the Prussian military, the German citizen with his incomparable "industriousness," capitalism, trade and

entrepreneurship, in short, Kaiser Wilhelm's Germany, which approached the zenith of
its glamor at the turn of the century—began to be surrounded with a curious religious
halo.[12]

Without explicitly using the term, Barth here portrays what Niebuhr
systematizes as the orientation of Culture-Protestantism. In the person of
Naumann the prevailing patterns of nineteenth-century theology are
condemned because they uncritically reflect the cultural trends of the day.

In part because of the influence of Barth's judgment, the voices of the
condemned themselves have for several generations too seldom been heard in
their own right. The result has been twofold. On the one hand, significant
continuities between Neo-orthodoxy and its predecessors in the tradition of
theological liberalism have been insufficiently emphasized. And on the other
hand, the inchoate but remarkably coherent alternative to Neo-orthodoxy
that is represented most impressively in the thought of Ernst Troeltsch has not
received the attention it deserves. In the following historical exposition and
systematic analysis, I attempt to redress this double deficiency. My intention
is to allow the multiple voices that have too often been silenced with the
epithet "Culture-Protestantism" to become audible again. As is already
evident in my formulation of the deficiencies to be redressed, I am, however,
especially intrigued with the voice of Troeltsch. His thought figures
prominently in the exposition and analysis in the first instance because I find
his writings consistently insightful in focusing distinctions among theological
positions at the turn of the century. But there is also another consideration
that his central role in the following discussion reflects. It is that in my view
Troeltsch articulates the most viable approach to the questions which his
generation has bequeathed to the successors of Neo-orthodoxy.

2   The Ritschlians and the History of Religions School

Both the anticipations of and the alternatives to Neo-orthodoxy are represented most concertedly at the turn of the twentieth century in those traditions that trace their lineage through Albrecht Ritschl. It is worth noting that Ritschl himself and his immediate followers self-consciously rejected the designation "liberal." Though they characterized their thought as modern in contrast to the so-called positive theology of the pietists and conservatives, they also insisted that their program was distinct from and systematically opposed to what they considered theological liberalism—namely the so-called speculative rationalism of thinkers like A. E. Biedermann and Otto Pfleiderer. More willing to acknowledge their common ground with the liberals were the youngest offspring of Ritschlianism, who came to be identified as the religionsgeschichtliche Schule (the historical approach to the study of religions, usually translated, not without a change in nuance, as the history of religions school). This difference both in nomenclature and in orientation toward liberalism is, moreover, representative of a range of issues between the older and younger Ritschlians that illustrates the diversity, the complexity, and the intensity of controversy within the theology against which Neo-orthodoxy targeted its attack.

2.1   The Varieties of Ritschlianism

The weekly newspaper/journal in which the exchange between Barth and Harnack transpired is a convenient point of reference for focusing distinctions in what is more or less self-consciously blurred together in references to late nineteenth-century theological liberalism. The *Christliche Welt* issued its trial number in November 1886 and began regular publication in 1887, for the first year with the name *Evangelical Lutheran Congregational Newspaper for the Educated Members of the Protestant Churches*. Founded by four of Harnack's students in Leipzig—Wilhelm Bornemann, Paul Drews, Friedrich Loofs, and Martin Rade—the journal quickly became a leading forum for theological discussion.

The person who most influenced the *Christliche Welt* was Rade, who served as its editor from its founding until 1932. During the first years of its publication, Rade worked as a pastor in a small village near Dresden where he was engaged from the completion of his studies in 1882 until 1892. In that year he moved to another pastorate in Frankfurt, which he held until 1900. In Frankfurt Rade was actively involved in social and political issues both on his own and together with Friedrich Naumann, who was his brother-in-law.

Through his intellectual interests, ecclesiastical affiliations, and social-political activities, Rade brought to his editorship of the *Christliche Welt* an awareness of a broad range of contemporary issues to which he sought to have authors in the journal relate Christian faith. This concern continued when Rade accepted an academic appointment in Marburg and moved the publication with him in 1900.

The excitement and the attractiveness of this world of the *Christliche Welt* is well-attested—by none other than Karl Barth, who worked as Rade's editorial assistant in Marburg in 1908 and 1909. In a 1947 letter to Rade's biographer, Johannes Rathje, Barth records his impressions of that time:

> At that time a full year's production of liberal or as one said then "modern" theology one way or another went through my hands. . . . Everything that I got to see and hear in these surroundings had such a taken-for-granted sparkle—this world, embodied in so many able and gifted [geistvollen] figures, revolved in so self-assured a fashion—that I surely would have only laughed at and ridiculed anyone who would have predicted that my future could lie in any direction other than a continuation of the theology of Marburg and specifically of the *Christliche Welt.*[13]

But for Barth this world in its entirety also died with World War I:

> I had to have once lived this fully . . . in the atmosphere and in the spirit of that twilight of the Schleiermacherian era, I had to have yet once more turned to it with my whole youthful trust, in order to be allowed to discover some seven years later that this era now really needed to have come to an end.[14]

The *Christliche Welt* is, then, a microcosm of that era of nineteenth-century theology that Barth saw as hopelessly compromised in its legitimation of pre-war culture. Accordingly, the profound conflicts and tensions within this circle merit more careful attention than they usually receive.

Under Rade's editorship, the *Christliche Welt* made a concerted effort to reflect a spectrum of theological and ecclesiastical positions. But its initial role was that of an organ for expressing the views of Ritschl's students, especially those who were themselves by then on theological faculties. By the 1870s the Ritschlians had gained considerable prominence in German academic theology and by the 1880s they were consolidating their position. In Göttingen, Halle, Giessen, Marburg, Tübingen, and Berlin, Ritschlians exercised more and more influence. Wilhelm Herrmann and Adolf Harnack were no doubt the best known; but Julius Kaftan, Johannes Gottschick, Ferdinand Kattenbusch, H. H. Wendt, Max Reischle, Otto Kirn, Otto Ritschl, and Friedrich Traub along with Bornemann, Drews, Loofs, and such older scholars as Theodore Häring and Hermann Schultz were also associated with the views or so-called school of Ritschl. The Ritschlians of course used other media as well. In 1876 the Ritschl-influenced New Testament scholar Emil Schürer founded the *Theologische Literaturzeitung* and in 1891 Gottschick initiated the *Zeitschrift für Theologie und Kirche.* But the

Christiliche Welt along with its monograph series, its organized circle of friends, and its annual meetings nonetheless was a central forum and barometer first of theological Ritschlianism and then in time of the debates between this older generation and the younger scholars of the history of religions school. Those debates focused on the thought of Johannes Weiss and Ernst Troeltsch. But also included on the side of the challengers were Wilhelm Bousset, Herrmann Gunkel, Albert Eichhorn, William Wrede, Wilhelm Heitmüller, and Paul Wernle.

In reporting the deep divisions among the supporters of and contributors to the *Christliche Welt* from 1893 on, Rathje has assembled quotations from correspondence that document an intense struggle between theological generations.[15] Loofs, Kaftan, and Kattenbusch complain to Rade about the "radicalism" of Weiss and Troeltsch in particular. In the letters and in Rade's responses, the issue is explicitly formulated as one between the older and the younger members. When the first serious complaints emerge after Weiss's 1893 address to the organization of supporters of the journal on the topic of the present situation of the church, Rade identifies with the older group in his correspondence. But in the ensuing few years Rade came more and more to think that only the younger contributors were grappling with contemporary issues. Accordingly, he resisted attempts in 1895 and 1896 to exclude Weiss from the organization and finally resigned himself to losing the support of many of the older members in order to retain the interest and allegiance of those like Weiss, Bousset, Troeltsch, and Wrede who were characterized as on the theological left (Linksstehenden).

The older Ritschlians were not, of course, without internal divisions among themselves. Kaftan and Herrmann may serve to illustrate the range of differences. Kaftan is unusual (though not exceptional, since Kirn and Reischle also evidence this tendency) among the older Ritschlians in his willingness to order Christianity into the history of religions as a whole. In his *Essence of the Christian Religion,* for example, he appropriates historical and comparative data about non-Christian as well as Christian traditions as the foundation for his exposition of Christian dogmatics.[16] In contrast, Herrmann (like Harnack in his constructive theological work and to a lesser extent Gottschick) focuses his theology more sharply than Ritschl himself on the person of Jesus as distinguished from even closely related Christian traditions about his life and ministry.[17] More remarkable still is the difference between Kaftan and Herrmann in their respective appraisals of mysticism. For Kaftan the mystical dimension of religious life has a central authority. For him it has priority over even the ethical—a position for which he was subject to criticism not only from other Ritschlians but also from Ritschl himself.[18] On this issue, despite his own pietistic background and experiential orientation, Herrmann reflects the characteristic Ritschlian position about the potentially debilitating ethical effects of mysticism. In *The Communion of the Christian with God,* for example, he is concerned to distinguish his interpretation of communion or intercourse, with its emphasis on the believer's historical experience of God in Christ, from traditional, especially Roman Catholic, mysticism. [19] As a correlate of this disparate appraisal of mysticism, Kaftan and Herrmann also differ in their interpretation of the religious status of secular activity. In Kaftan a definite and self-conscious other-worldliness is affirmed. [20] In contrast, Herrmann shares the concern of Ritschl himself to avoid any such subordination of ethical existence in history to a future life. [21]

Despite such not insignificant differences among the older Ritschlians, there is, however, still systematic common ground that helps to account for their united opposition to the younger scholars of the history of religions school. This shared orientation is most evident in their agreement as to the central significance of what they all affirm as the unique historical revelation in Christ. At this point their common commitment to at least portions of the Synoptic Gospels, to Luther, and to Kant converge. The primacy of practical reason, the indispensability of grace through faith, and the canon within the canon (however drastically reduced) all meet in the affirmation of God's revelation to the believer in the historical person of Jesus. This revelation of God as other—a revelation that, they insist, can occur only at the divine initiative through grace and that is not available to the knowledge and control of theoretical or speculative reason—is what distinguishes Christianity from all other religious and cultural traditions. It is what Christian faith is in the end about for all the Ritschlians. [22]

A critical presupposition of this Ritschlian program is that there is a virtual identity between contemporary Christian affirmation and divine revelation in the first century. The faith of the contemporary Christian must after all affirm what is revealed in the historical Jesus. In time Ritschlians like Kaftan and Herrmann and Harnack came to see that this presupposition was neither as self-evident nor as necessary as Ritschl's own formulations suggest. But granting refinements in conceptualization, what are presented as data about the divine revelation in the historical Jesus continue to constitute the sole explicit authority to which the Ritschlians appeal in commending the religious and ethical injunctions of Christian faith.

The approach of the history of religions school poses a systematic threat to the Ritschlian program because it calls into question precisely this appeal and the presupposition on which it is grounded. Criticism at this point was not, to be sure, unprecedented. For example, Otto Pfleiderer, the liberal who consistently opposed Ritschlianism and who was the only member of the Berlin theological faculty to vote against Harnack's invitation to teach there, caustically attacks what he describes as the combination of "moralistic rationalism and dogmatic positivism" that results from this "all too naive interpretation" for which "the 'revelation of God in Jesus' . . . is an immediately certain and generally understandable fact." [23] But such attacks from the left served only to counterbalance opposition to Ritschlianism on the right—until criticism in effect dissolved the school from within.

The publication of Weiss's *Jesus' Proclamation of the Kingdom of God* in 1892 documents this process of internal dissolution. Weiss was not only one of Ritschl's students but also his son-in-law. His book focuses on what is perhaps the most characteristic concept or image for Ritschlian theology: the kingdom of God. Weiss's own theological stance is, moreover, very appreciative of theological attention to this motif, as his opening sentence indicates:

> One of the most gratifying and promising aspects of recent theology is the serious attention to and emphasis upon the concept "Kingdom of God."[24]

Yet despite this sympathy with the concerns of Ritschl's theological program, Weiss fundamentally, even if only implicitly, calls into question the entire structure of authority on which that program was based.

Weiss comments in his preface that he drafted the essay "some time ago." That he did not publish the book until three years after Ritschl's death suggests his own awareness of the radicality of the critique he advances. In any case, his understated summary trenchantly formulates the central issue:

> But this conception of ours of the βασιλεία τοῦ θεοῦ parts company with Jesus' at the most decisive point. *We* do not mean the religious side of this concept antithetically, as the counterpart to αἰων οὗτος, but merely thetically: it expresses our belief that God the Creator maintains his control *over this world,* and governs it for the spiritual benefit of his children. Its ethical side is thoroughly unbiblical and un-Jewish, inasmuch as the notion of an "actualization of the Rule of God" by human ethical activity is completely contrary to the transcendentalism of Jesus' idea. Under these circumstances, one will perhaps judge the connection of the modern dogmatic idea with the words of Jesus to be a purely external one. This is, in fact, the case. That which is universally valid in Jesus' preaching, which should form the kernel of our systematic theology, is not his idea of the Kingdom of God, but that of the religious and ethical fellowship of the children of God. This is not to say that one ought no longer to use the concept "Kingdom of God" in the current manner. On the contrary, it seems to me, as a matter of fact, that it should be the proper watchword of modern theology. Only the admission must be demanded that we use it in a different sense from Jesus'.[25]

Involved here are basic methodological questions of norms and procedures, as Weiss makes clear in the metaphor with which he closes his introductory remarks:

> Theology must insist only on one thing if it wants to remain clear concerning itself and conscious of its procedures, namely, that one should acknowledge whether and how far we today are removed from the original meaning of the concepts, and that one should declare, for the sake of clarity, that he wishes to issue the old coinage at a new rate of exchange.[26]

Weiss's sixty-seven page essay is, then, a signal for the end of a theological epoch because of its impact on formal questions rather than because of the specific content of its theology. Indeed, Weiss himself declares his allegiance to central tenets of Ritschlian theology. Yet his insistence—along with that of Wrede and, a decade later, of Albert Schweitzer—on the "eschatalogical attitude" of primitive Christianity demonstrates the untenability of claims for a virtual identity between the proclamation of Jesus and Ritschlian theology. Accordingly, it focuses the need for attention to the problems of authority and theological method that Ritschlianism sought to solve through the assertion of this identity.

2.2   Ernst Troeltsch and "Historical Method"

Weiss himself does not address such formal issues in detail. Instead, the Ritschlian theological allegiances expressed in his 1893 essay are even more evident in his subsequent writings. In an 1895 book on Christian discipleship, for example, Weiss criticizes both Herrmann and Kaftan explicitly. But in the first case, he invokes the authority of Ritschl himself to counter Herrmann's conception of the relationship between faith and the historical Jesus; and in the second case he employs the Ritschlian dichotomy between nature and culture in resisting Kaftan's analysis.[27] Similarly, in his *The Idea of the Kingdom of God in Theology,* Weiss concludes his historical treatment with a discussion of Ritschlian theology into which he merges his own constructive position.[28] Weiss does insist that intellectual honesty requires the recognition of the fundamental differences between Jesus' preaching and (as he became convinced through his further research) virtually all subsequent theology from the New Testament on; he does not, however, argue against the Ritschlian theological framework as such.

Troeltsch's approach stands in contrast to the tendency of Weiss to focus on the similarities between his own position and that of at least Ritschl himself. With a flair for the dramatic, Troeltsch accentuates the differences between the Ritschlians and "the younger generation." The *Christliche Welt* once again provides a convenient illustration, in this case of the increasingly self-conscious divisions evident by the end of the 1890s. The occasion for debate was the publication of a book on the theology of Ritschl and his followers. In 1897 a pastor in Bremen named Gustav Ecke published *The Theological School of Albrecht Ritschl.* In September 1897 Harnack reviewed the book favorably. Then followed, in January 1898, a further review by Kattenbusch. And then in July 1898 Troeltsch replied to Kattenbusch's review.

Ecke's book and each of the reviews note the tensions within the so-called Ritschlian school. Ecke's own interest centers on those tendencies in Ritschlian theology which move toward more common ground with an "unabbreviated Biblical-Reformation confession of faith."[29] Häring is his most frequent example; but on various points Gottschick, Kattenbusch, Loofs, Bornemann, Herrmann, and even Reischle, Rade, and Harnack himself are cited as correctives to Ritschl's own position. This entire generation of theologians is contrasted to the younger "Ritschlian left" which in Ecke's view includes Wrede, Gunkel, Baldensperger, Weiss and Bousset but is most self-consciously represented in Troeltsch.[30] In his review, Harnack notes this left-right distinction only in passing, but he also observes that in his judgment Ecke overestimates the contemporary apologetic power of the Ritschlian program because he does not recognize "the plethora of burdensome questions" which Ritschl managed to evade but which must be confronted before long.[31] In contrast to both Harnack's reference to the need for exploring fundamental issues that have been avoided and his reticence about the conflicts between the so-called right and left wings of the school, Kattenbusch's review calls emphatic attention to what is praised as Ecke's correct perception of "two streams among the Ritschlians." Kattenbusch concurs in his inclusion among the "older" and "more conservative" members of the movement and then proceeds to dissociate himself from the "younger" group. He focuses in particular on Troeltsch, who he says in the end denies the supernatural character of Christianity out of his "need to be modern."[32] To this attack Troeltsch then replied explicity as a representative of the "younger generation" in an article entitled "On the Theological Situation."

Echoing a theme which Harnack adumbrated in his review, Troeltsch argues that the success of Ritschl's program was dependent on the cultural situation of the 1850s during which it emerged: a time of disenchantment with the speculative systems of the first half of the century combined with a sense of self-evident assurance, which was itself at least in part based on those very systems, as to the absoluteness or the finality of Christianity. This ethos was very hospitable toward Ritschl's theology, with its emphatically anti-speculative rhetoric and ostensibly empirical grounding in the service of a strict supernaturalism.[33] "But in the meantime," Troeltsch observes, "cultural life as a whole has not stood still." In general, there has been a shift of intellectual interest and resources from speculative philosophy to historical and analytical studies. Specifically in theology, Troeltsch maintains pointedly, there has been a movement of influence and talent from dogmatic to historical concerns. More specifically still, the attempt of the Ritschlians to "push away" historical problems through the expedient of dichotomies between Christianity and other religions, between natural and supernatural revelation, has collapsed. Hence there has emerged from within the Ritschlian movement a re-assertion of those criticisms that from the beginning questioned the isolation of Christianity from the whole of history and from the methods applied to all other historical traditions.[34]

Similarly unequivocal but more detailed in the contrast it depicts is Troeltsch's essay on "Historical and Dogmatic Method in Theology," also published in 1898. This essay was written in response to an article very critical of Troeltsch written by one of Kaftan's students, Friedrich Niebergall, and entitled "On the Absoluteness of Christianity." (Troeltsch's own lecture/essay with that title appeared four years later.) But the response is also presented as Troeltsch's "final word" in a series of exchanges with Kaftan himself. That series of exchanges occured in the *Zeitschrift für Theologie und Kirche;* it includes Troeltsch's two part essay on "The Independence of Religion" in 1895 and 1896, Kaftan's response under the title of "The Independence of Christianity" in 1896, Troeltsch's "History and Metaphysics" in 1898 and Kaftan's "Reply: (1) Method; (2) Supernaturalism" in the same issue. As the title to his 1898 response suggests, Kaftan charges Troeltsch with confusing substantive and methodological questions. Kaftan acknowledges that he distinguishes God's revelation as different in kind from whatever revelation may occur in other traditions and affirms this Biblical revelation as supernatural. But he insists that this substantive disagreement with Troeltsch does not constitute or entail a difference in method.[35] "Historical and Dogmatic Method in Theology" is, then, Troeltsch's response to this contention.

Troeltsch maintains that Niebergall in particular and the established theology of the time in general display a persistent tendency to focus on specific problems raised by historical criticism without addressing the underlying systematic issues involved—to use his words, "the much deeper ground where the disintegration of the Christian complex of ideas actually originates." Troeltsch locates this "deeper ground" in the "historical method simply as such" which is "a leaven that transforms everything and finally explodes the very form of earlier theological methods."[36] Accordingly, he wants to demonstrate how this historical method is in principle different from and opposed to not only "the old dogmatic method" but also such attenuated forms of dogmatics as those represented in Ritschlianism. To this end, he provides a cursory description of historical method and then formulates the implications for theology so as to contrast them with the procedures of the dogmatic approach.

Troeltsch maintains that historical criticism makes any specific or isolated fact uncertain and problematical in itself because it cannot be separated either from the present of the interpreter or from its own historical context. Accordingly, "the connection between religious faith and all particular facts is loosened":

> To be sure, the connection is not broken, but its character is changed. Now it becomes impossible to base religious faith on any single fact: faith and fact are linked by large and broad connections: their relationship is mediate, not direct.[37]

Nor does attention to a single complex and developing tradition suffice:

> It follows from the univocity and the total interconnection of historical events that their evaluation and judgment no less than their explanation and description must take their starting point from the total context. . . . No just estimate of Christianity can be formed except by reference to the total context—even as the self-judgment of the Greeks or the Romans cannot be allowed to determine our estimate of their permanent contribution to the human spirit.[38]

In characteristic understatement, Troeltsch argues that the dogmatic method is "in principle and absolutely opposed" to this comparative and critical starting point. In contrast to historical method, the dogmatic approach "starts from a point of origin completely beyond the relativity of history" and then "seeks to commit people to certain particular facts of history, and indeed just those facts that demonstrate the character of its authority as destroying every historical analogy."[39] Troeltsch grants that much of recent dogmatics stresses the "historical" and "factual" character of Christianity for apologetic purposes:

> To be sure, it too claims to be based on "history." But this is not the ordinary, secular history, like that of critical historiography. It is rather a salvation history, a nexus of saving facts which, as such, are knowable and provable only to the eyes of faith.[40]

Troeltsch maintains that this position merely substitutes the notion of an inaccessible salvation history with its own special methodologies for the category of the miraculous in traditional dogmatics. As such, it still represents the dogmatic method, though in a form which sensitivity to historical criticism has thoroughly vitiated and compromised. To quote his own colorful metaphor:

> Contemporary dogmatic theologians . . . believe that they can pluck fruit without having a tree or . . . after cutting a small, dry twig from an old trunk, expect fruit to grow from this twig.[41]

The common commitment of the Ritschlians to grounding theology in the unique historical revelation in Christ is, then, in Troeltsch's view still an instance of dogmatic method. Such concessions to historical criticism as a theologian like Niebergall makes serve only to deprive traditional dogmatics of its power without recasting its pattern of authority. Accordingly, this position can at most serve as a transition to a systematically and thoroughly historical method. This method must in Troeltsch's view attend to patterns or regularities that are evident over time and across traditions. In this sense, it must take as its starting point the most comprehensive attainable context rather than isolated facts or even one discrete tradition.[42]

3 Christ and Cult

In his essay on historical and dogmatic method, Troeltsch elaborates two ideal types so as to accentuate the differences between the program of the history of religions school and that of the older Ritschlians. The result is no doubt a significant systematic contrast—between the procedures of traditional orthodoxy and the method that Troeltsch advocates. But that leaves the question of the extent to which it illumines significant continuing differences among liberal or so-called modern theologians apart from typological exaggerations. To answer this question, a further look is required at specific substantive debates of the period with reference both to the theological interpretation and the cultural analysis involved.

3.1 The Jesus of History and the Christ of Faith

Troeltsch was not alone in noting the special character of the history in which Christian theology, as represented in Ritschlian dogmatics, claimed to be grounded. Nor did his criticism of this conception of a discrete salvation history go unchallenged. Indeed, from the 1890s on the allegedly special character of the history that grounds Christian faith became a renewed focus for systematic attention in apologetic efforts from multiple points on the theological spectrum. One indication of this greater self-consciousness about the claim that theology is based in history is the increasing currency of a formalized distinction between "historisch" and "geschlichtlich" in theological discussion. Allowing for some variation in specific formulations, there was general agreement among those who employed this distinction that historisch refers to what can be known with confidence through critical historical scholarship while geschichtlich indicates past events that influence the present whether or not they are recoverable in detail by the historian.

A programmatic and influential example of the use of this distinction is Martin Kähler's *The So-called Historical (historiche) Jesus and the Historical (geschichtliche) Biblical Christ*, which appeared in 1892. The title already conveys Kähler's thesis: the past figure which historical and historiographical scholarship strives to recover (in vain, because the sources are not reliable according to the accepted canons of the discipline) and the Christ of faith are "two fundamentally different things." Kähler elaborates this contention so as to argue for the need to include the entire Biblical witness as the foundation for theology. In particular, he criticizes those Ritschlians who like Herrmann in effect canonize only a selection from the New Testament.[43] In short, Kähler employs the geschichtlich/historisch distinction to defend so-called positive theology over against more liberal positions.

25

This defense of positive theology is not, however, the only use to which the geschichtlich/historisch distinction was put. Instead, it was also pressed into service to commend the Ritschlian program. An extended illustration of this appropriation of the geschichtlich/historisch distinction for Ritschlian theology is provided in an essay that Reischle published in 1897 under the title "The Controversy Concerning the Grounding of Faith on the 'Historical' Jesus Christ." In this essay Reischle uses the geschichtlich/historisch terminology in order to indicate a double tendency or meaning in the shared Ritschlian commitment to grounding dogmatics on the historical revelation in Jesus Christ. He formulates the two tendencies concisely: for the first one, "dogmatics must seek its foundation and norm in the historical (geschicht-lichen)—that is, disciplined historiographical (wissenschaftlich historis-chen)—understanding of God's revelation in the actions, teachings, and suffering of Jesus Christ"; and for the second one dogmatics "must build on a faith-apprehension of the historical (geschichtlichen) revelation."[44] Reischle himself prefers the second position and argues that this preference allows the genuine differences between the Ritschlians and their opponents to emerge more clearly than if the distinction is not made. So, for example, he is able to agree with Kähler that it is not only impossible but also unnecessary to get "behind" the New Testament witness to the "real historical Jesus"; but at the same time he can retain the Ritschlian emphasis on "revelation in Christ" as a criterion for making judgments among Biblical traditions over against the insistence of positive theology that they are all to be regarded as equally valuable.[45] Similarly, Reischle is able to counter the charges of Pfleiderer that Ritschlianism entails both authoritarianism and positivism in its fixation on allegedly objective external occurrences; yet he can still resist the liberal-rationalist claim that the historical Jesus is irrelevant to religious truth through the Ritschlian affirmation that the apprehension of faith is grounded in an historical revelation.[46]

It is noteworthy that in both the Kähler and the Reischle essays the Ritschlian who most consistently attracts attention is Herrmann. His sharp focusing of the conception of revelation on the person of Jesus Christ invites Kähler's attack that too much of the Biblical testimony is relegated to a peripheral status and Reischle's defense that a definite and clear criterion over against the tradition is enunciated. This exchange is in effect continued some years later with the publication of Georg Wobbermin's impressive essay, *Geschichte and Historie in the Study of Religion.* Wobbermin presents himself as a mediating theologian and outlines his own position as between those of Kähler and Herrmann: over against the former, he thinks the judgments as to relative significance must be made among Biblical traditions; and in contrast to the latter, he is persuaded that the resurrection in particular must be included in the indispensable core because it is inseparable from the New Testament picture of Jesus. Wobbermin insists that he is not, however, interested simply in mediating between Kähler and Herrmann. Instead his concern is only to establish the need for and the utility in more strictly distinguishing between Geschichte and Historie than is usually the case.[47] From this perspective, Wobbermin carefully and systematically analyzes Herrmann's recent work to show that this distinction is not consistently observed. More specifically, he shows that Herrmann's discussions of "the fact of Jesus Christ" not infrequently trade on connotations of objective historical (historisch) reference, even though he at the same time denies emphatically that religious conviction is dependent on the judgments of historical research.[48]

Wobbermin's concern to protect faith from the results of historical criticism continues a perennial preoccupation of theology from the Enlightenment on. But the immediate occasion for his essay was the controversy that raged first in Germany but then also in England and America following the publication of Arthur Drews's *The Christ Myth* in 1909.[49] Drews was a Karlsruhe philosopher who conflated a variety of theories and items of research in the service of his own conviction that the religious philosophy of the future could and should dispense with Jesus. Drews combined pretensions to scholarship and indisputable skill as a publicist—with the result that the interest of church people and the resources of theologians were directed with remarkable if short-lived concentration to the unlikely question of whether or not Jesus ever existed at all. Public debates, church declarations, hundreds of reviews and journal articles, and dozens of books were the immediate result. The *Christliche Welt,* for example, regularly kept its readers informed of developments, published at least one church declaration (that of Bremen Protestants) on the issue, reviewed innumerable articles, speeches, and books, and devoted an entire number (that of February 17, 1910) to the issues involved. Other religious journals both in Germany and abroad displayed similar if less extensive interest. And despite their disdain for Drews's methods both as a scholar and as a sensationalizer, leading theologians both in Germany and abroad addressed the questions that he brought to widespread public attention.

Of particular interest with reference to the issues that Wobbermin's essay focuses are the contributions of Herrmann and Troeltsch to the debate. There is a remarkable measure of common ground among Wobbermin, Reischle, Herrmann, and Troeltsch—to name them in order from positive enthusiasm to negative criticism on the question of the usefulness of the formalized distinction between Geschichte and Historie. In addressing the question of the significance of Jesus, all four focus on the need to articulate an alternative both to a positivistically historical orientation (whether of the left or the right) that claims to be based exclusively on verifiable past events and to the position of speculative rationalism that relies on general truths and is indifferent to all historical processes. The interest of both Reischle and Wobbermin in contrasting Geschichte to Historie is their confidence that the distinction provides resources for conceptualizing this third position. In Herrmann's case, the alternatives are most frequently named positive and liberal theology.[50] And in Troeltsch's terminology, the positions to be avoided are those classified as historisch-factual and pedagogical-symbolic.[51] The specific formulations and the particular figures on whom discussion focuses are, to be sure, not identical. But there is nonetheless a shared general recognition of the desirability, indeed the necessity, of a position that is neither ahistorical in the sense of rationalistic liberalism nor positivistically historical in the mode of either literalistic theological conservatism or reductionistic empiricism.

In this their own chosen frame of reference, the line of argument which Reischle and Wobbermin advance is much more vulnerable than their confident rhetoric suggests. The difficulties are especially evident in Wobbermin's attempt to apply the Geschichte/Historie distinction with relentless consistency. After discussing the positions of Kähler and Herrmann, Wobbermin turns to Bousset's contribution to the Christ-myth debate for his final illustration of the need to distinguish between Geschichte and Historie. Bousset's essay becomes Wobbermin's example of that tradition of liberal rationalism strongly indebted to Kant. Accordingly, this culminating case in his analysis allows Wobbermin to focus the differences between the position he advocates and the two alternatives he rejects:

> On the whole, then, there is this to say about the significance of history (Geschichte) for religion: history does not, to be sure, provide the demonstration of religious truth, but it also does not simply provide illustrations of that truth; rather history provides the invention of religious truth. It is the unavoidable and enduring condition for the faithful grasping of religious truth.[52]

That Kant himself in *Religion Within the Limits of Reason Alone* repeatedly refers to positive religion as the "necessary vehicle" of rational faith already indicates the central question that Wobbermin's analysis unintentionally raises—namely, whether the simple expedient of introducing the Geschichte/ Historie distinction succeeds in satisfactorily conceptualizing the differences between his allegedly historical position and the ahistorical orientation of rationalism. And doubt on this score is only reinforced when Wobbermin concludes his essay with the assertion that "faith would be able to accept with equanimity even the negative answer to the question of the historicity of Jesus Christ."[53]

The issue here is not (at least in the first instance) whether Wobbermin's (and Reischle's) use of the Geschichte/Historie distinction is itself viable but rather whether this distinction is successful in articulating an alternative to the liberal rationalism it is attempting to oppose. This issue is focused with specific reference to the positions of Herrmann and Troeltsch in an essay published in the *Zeitschrift für Theologie und Kirche* in 1912. The author, Wilhelm Fresenius, aligns himself with Herrmann and explicitly invokes the Geschichte/Historie distinction as Wobbermin defines it in order to criticize the argument that Troeltsch advances in his 1911 essay, *The Significance of the Historicity of Jesus for Faith.* Fresenius charges Troeltsch with a "historische perspective" that fails to appreciate the "third possibility"—namely "that something is significant for us because it is historically (geschichtlich) effective."[54] Even to establish a verbal contrast between his own position and that of the liberal rationalists he opposes, Fresenius has to rephrase Troeltsch's "pedagogical-symbolic" classification so that it refers to positions which base significance only on the "rationally understandable." But if the issue involves more than a rhetorical contrast, it is not clear how the position Fresenius defends is different in substance from the liberal rationalism of a Kant or a Strauss or a Biedermann or a Pfleiderer, since surely such figures also want to affirm that images or ideas or symbols or principles must affect persons, must exhibit historical efficacy, to be significant.

3.2   The Historical Jesus and the Cultic Christ

The remarkable achievement of Troeltsch's lecture/essay on the significance of the historicity (Geschichtlichkeit!) of Jesus for faith is that it advances the discussion on precisely this issue on which the Ritschlians and their apologists (Reischle, Wobbermin, and Fresenius) focus while at the same time specifying the intention of Herrmann's position more accurately than do his defenders. Troeltsch is, to be sure, quite critical of Herrmann's views. He uses the scarcely complimentary rubric "hybrids" ("Mischformen") to characterize the efforts of the Schleiermacher-Ritschl-Herrmann tradition in theology to find a middle ground between the Enlightenment and orthodoxy, between the rationalism of the liberals and historical particularity.[55] He accompanies this pejorative designation with the contention that this entire theological tradition continues to reflect at least the remnants of an orthodox exclusivism or absolutism which historical scrutiny not only of Biblical but also of comparative historical data no longer allows. In the case of Herrmann in particular, Troeltsch sees this tendency in his insistent connection of faith to the historical personality of Christ. He argues that Herrmann's position at this point is reminiscent of Schleiermacher's affirmation of the sinlessness of Christ, which Strauss criticizes so mercilessly. And in Troeltsch's view such unqualified Christocentrism is a no longer tenable position because its presupposition is the orthodox affirmation of a once-for-all atonement. It is, to use his characteristically provocative metaphor, "for religion what geocentrism and anthropocentrism are for cosmology and metaphysics."[56] Yet despite much sharp criticism, Troeltsch self-consciously advances his own interpretation as an attempt to execute what he sees as the underlying program of Schleiermacher, Ritschl, and Herrmann more consistently than they do themselves.

After his survey of the hybrid position that he argues Schleiermacher, Ritschl, and Herrmann illustrate, Troeltsch observes that for those who cannot accept the orthodox belief in supernatural atonement, "there remains, then, nothing except a pure historisch-factual and a pedagogical-symbolic meaning of the person of Jesus"—to which he himself responds that at this prospect, "a quiet chill comes over one."[57] This apprehension is, Troeltsch argues, grounded in the realization that individual appropriation of past facts or interpretation of ever present symbols neither generates nor even satisfactorily conducts religious power. Instead, religious efficacy is dependent on the vitality of a historical community that centers on a particular cult—dependent, in short, on precisely those energies that so-called modern religiosity blocks through its rationalism and individualism.[58]

Thus Troeltsch agrees with Reischle, Wobbermin, Fresenius, and Herrmann not only that a third alternative to speculative rationalism and historical positivism is required but also that an appreciation of the historical significance of Jesus constitutes that third alternative. In contrast to Reischle, Wobbermin, and Fresenius, his description of this third position is, however, so specified that its difference from the alternatives does not depend on questionable verbal distinctions like the one between Historie and Geschichte. And in contrast to Herrmann's insistence on direct personal encounter with the historical Jesus, Troeltsch focuses on the social-psychological dynamics through which the figure of Christ is both central to and indispensable for the cultic life of the Christian community.[59]

In his formulation of this contrast to Herrmann's position, the methodological commitments expressed in the essay on historical and dogmatic method are exemplified. The connection between faith and fact cannot in Troeltsch's view be a direct one—as in the at least tacit analogy to immediate encounter between one person and another. Instead he grounds the historical significance of Jesus for faith in general social-psychological requirements applicable to multiple traditions. But he at the same time calls attention to what he thinks is justified in Herrmann's apparently unintelligible talk about the fact of Christ. In contrast to the tendency entailed in a consistent Geschichte/Historie distinction, Troeltsch sees the thrust of Herrmann's position precisely in its insistence on the concrete historical reality, facticity, actuality of the personality of Jesus—an insistence which setting geschichtlich over against historisch unavoidably compromises in the direction of "mere" images or ideas or symbols or principles.[60] It is, in short, not simply carelessness on Herrmann's part that his references to the fact of Jesus Christ do not conform to the Geschichte/Historie distinction that Wobbermin employs so effectively for analytical purposes. Rather it is consistent with Herrmann's self-conscious procedure over a period of some thirty years to minimize the threat of Biblical criticism through concentration on the inner life or the person of Jesus as having direct resonance with the believer's own experience in the present. It is, therefore, not surprising that Herrmann's 1913 contribution to the Christ-myth debate still does not use the Geschichte/Historie contrast as Kähler, Reischle, Wobbermin, Fresenius and others commend it. He does, to be sure, as always maintain that faith must be based on the experience of Christ—not on historical reports.[61] But he also acknowledges that faith cannot be completely secure from the results of historical research:

> What lives in history can be nourished through historical research—but 'it can also be threatened by it. . . . Genuine Christian faith should simply reflect on the way in which it lives not only in but also from history. Then the danger will never, to be sure, be put aside, but rather ever again overcome.[62]

Insofar as Herrmann's recurrent references to the fact of Jesus Christ indicate his commitment to relating Christian faith to the historical actuality of the founder, Troeltsch registers his agreement. Indeed, he maintains that his focus on the social-psychological requirements of religious cult and community serves to underscore this necessity for Jesus' historicity. In this connection, Troeltsch castigates the "aestheticizing play" that expects believers to nourish their religious needs with a "mythical symbol." He grants that in other contexts—the West before the eighteenth century, for example—problems need not arise in the connection. But for believing communities as they actually exist in the historical consciousness of the post-Enlightenment West, Troeltsch is convinced that completely negative conclusions on the questions of the "historicity" or "knowability" of Jesus would be "the beginning of the end of the Christ-symbol":

> For one who really intensely belongs to the Christian life-world, it is impossible to hold the center and head of the community, the focus of the whole cult and of all intuitions of God, as simply a myth—no matter how beautiful the myth.[63]

Hence Troeltsch concurs with what he takes to be the intention of Herrmann's references to the fact of Jesus Christ and is persuaded that what is all but unintelligible in his personalistic terminology is both comprehensible and crucial if the historical Jesus is recognized as the originating figure in the developing cultic tradition that has Christ at its center.

Because of his concern to counter what he terms "aestheticizing play" that insists on satisfaction with myths or symbols alone, Troeltsch in this essay on occasion sounds like the historical positivists to whom he is eqully opposed. Indeed, in his already cited essay on the Christ-myth debate, B. A. Gerrish characterizes Troeltsch's position on this issue as "a drastic stand which stakes everything on knowledge of the historical Jesus" and assigns "decisive significance to the question of origins—understood as the question of correspondence between the symbol and Jesus as he actually was."[64] Here Gerrish's exposition exaggerates even Troeltsch's most extreme formulations—and then expresses puzzlement at the apparent dissonance with other Troeltschian commitments. It is arguable that Troeltsch is excessively sanguine about the reliability of New Testament documents. In any case, he does consider the historicity and knowability of the main outlines of Jesus' personality and preaching to be virtually assured and as a result may claim that more must be known about the founder than his own position actually requires.[65] But he never speaks of "correspondence between the symbol and Jesus as he actually was"; nor does he speak of "decisive significance" with respect to origins as somehow separate from subsequent development—as Gerrish himself observes in referring to the passages in which Troeltsch discusses both the broader historical context of questions about Jesus and the fact that even the earliest Christian community viewed the spirit of Christ as a "principle capable of development."[66]

What Troeltsch does maintain is that the historical Jesus and the cultic Christ are intimately and inextricably connected as origin and development—in contrast both to liberal rationalism and historical positivism. He sums up his position concisely and unmistakably in an essay written within a year of the one on the significance of the historicity of Jesus:

> It is no doubt possible to cultivate and to be active in the Christian world of ideas even without a specific connection precisely to Jesus. But in my opinion religiousness that bears within it the stuff of Christian faith will never cease centering its thoughts and assurances and hopes in the representation of this personality. With respect to this figure, it is then neither possible nor necessary to separate what he actually was and what the faith of millenia has lovingly projected onto him. No true religious community will be able to live from mere concepts and teachings, but will rather always want to apprehend them in living personalities. And among these, Jesus will always remain the strongest for the community, as long as it shares his faith at all. On this fact the whole cult is grounded; and a religion without a cult is no really vital religion.[67]

4 Christianity and Culture

Disagreements over the significance of Jesus focus the distinctions between the older Ritschlians and the history of religions school. The differences in approach illustrate alternative conceptions of the relationship between theology and other disciplines; and they also imply distinguishable positions as to the proper relationship of Christian practice to changing historical contexts. Interpretations of Christ and cult are, in short, correlative with analyses of the interaction between Christianity and culture. Accordingly, comparing and contrasting the two approaches to this complex of questions may serve to exemplify and at the same time to amplify the systematic issues involved.

4.1 Theology and the Disciplines

Commitment to the independence of theology over against the alleged imperialism of a changing array of academic disciplines has an intriguing and complex history among the Ritschlians. The opponent against which Ritschl himself directs his theology is a materialism that invokes the authority of the natural sciences on behalf of a closed system of causal explanation. Against this threat, he advances a teleological theological system that sharply contrasts spirit to nature so as to focus the imperative to realize the kingdom of God through historical development. This position, which despite its debt to Kant still is strongly under the influence of the Hegelian philosophy of history that Ritschl had earlier espoused, is represented in the first edition of *The Christian Doctrine of Justification and Reconciliation* (1870-1874). At this time Ritschl insists that the task of theology is the articulation of a disciplined theoretical defense of the practical certainty of faith in the divine governance of the world. As he puts it with reference to belief in God:

> This acceptance of the idea of God is no practical faith, but rather an act of theoretical cognition.[68]

In Herrmann's *Metaphysics in Theology* (1876), what is presented as the Ritschlian position is more sharply formulated in that metaphysics as such is identifed with the naturalistic and reductionistic materialism to which theology is opposed, a systematic opposition to metaphysics with which Ritschl publicly aligns himself in his *Theology and Metaphysics* (1881). A further refinement in specifying both the opponent of theology and the strategy for combat is evident in the increasing prominence of the conception of value judgments among the Ritschlians—first in Herrmann's *Religion in Relation to Cognition of the World and to Ethics* (1879), then in Kaftan's *The Essence of the Christian Religion* (1881), and finally in the second and third editions of Ritschl's work on justification and reconciliation (1883, 1888). Through a more thorough and explicit dependence on Kant, theology is distinguished not only from reductionistic metaphysics and the natural sciences but from all disciplines that aspire to attain theoretical knowledge. The contrast at least to the formulation of Ritschl's earlier position may be epitomized in the third edition revision of his remark about belief in God:

> This acceptance of the idea of God is, as Kant observes, practical faith and not an act of theoretical cognition.[69]

As is evident from even so cursory a survey of the development within Ritschlianism toward a systematic differentiation of theology from all theoretical disciplines, Herrmann was a consistent and influential proponent of movement in this direction. Indeed, Herrmann is ever more insistent on the need for this independence of theology from all theoretical knowledge and increasingly formulates his own position in contrast with what he views as Ritschl's less consistent approach. Herrmann's line of argument is expressed with particular clarity in a 1907 essay that specifies his position both as a further development of Ritschl's program and as a systematic alternative to the history of religions approach that he sees Troeltsch as representing.

In this essay, Herrmann takes as his point of departure "the gloomy picture of the past history and the current situation of Protestant dogmatics" that Troeltsch portrays in a 350 page contribution to the series *Kultur der Gegenwart*.[70] Herrmann indicates what he considers to be the historical and systematic error in Troeltsch's description and analysis. Historically, the error is said to be illustrated in and in part to derive from Troeltsch's emphasis on the discontinuities between sixteenth- and seventeenth-century thought and that of the Enlightenment. The result is what Herrmann views as an overstatement of the contrast between old and new Protestantism. This allegedly dubious historical description is in turn reflected in Troeltsch's commitment to establishing continuities between academic disciplines and religion—a commitment that expresses the Enlightenment preoccupation with the unity of reason.[71]

Along with his criticism of Troeltsch's presentation, Herrmann offers his alternative on both the systematic and the historical issues. The systematic contention is registered again and again: there is an irreducible distinction between religion and theoretical knowledge (Wissenschaft). Herrmann formulates this contention with explicit reference to Kant. But he also argues that the principle is central to Luther's theology. Indeed, he maintains that even Kant illustrates the mentality of the middle ages insofar as he tries to establish a general validity for religion in relation to ethics.[72] Against every such generalizing tendency, Herrmann asserts the radical particularity or individuality of religious experience that is entailed in the Lutheran affirmation of justification through faith alone. In support of this position he outlines the history of Protestant thought as a repeated compromising of Luther's central insight through the establishment of requirements for faith. Even Luther himself does not unambiguously reject a view of revelation as propositional and hence on occasion succumbs to the temptation to demand acceptance of scriptural authority. Schleiermacher reasserts the radical freedom of faith. But because the normative role of the Bible is not emphasized, the way is prepared for Ritschl's reassertion of scriptural authority—a reassertion which in turn must be criticized insofar as it establishes a new law over against the Gospel.[73]

In Herrmann's interpretation, Ritschl is the "last great representative of orthodox dogmatics," the thinker in whom "orthodox dogmatics found its most mature expression." This entire tradition is, however, no longer viable not only because its use of the Bible is untenable in the light of modern historical-critical exegesis but also because it in effect "makes the Holy Scriptures into a doctrinal requirement [Lehrgesetz]."[74] As a result, both the independence of theology and the uncompromised affirmation that justification is through faith alone demand the very position that Herrmann advocates: an unqualified rejection of all general or objective supports for religion in favor of a radically personal and experiential orientation.

In elaborating his position Herrmann acknowledges and attempts to meet the need for an interpretation of religion that is not confined to the Christian tradition. Especially in view of the fact that Rudolf Bultmann was among his students, Herrmann's formulations of this general interpretation of religion are very striking:

> The human being only has his own life if he can will the purpose that he serves as his own immutable end. . . . But then the independence of his own life becomes a task for him. . . . In this individual experience religion has its place; and here it attains truth.[75]

> Religion is nothing other than a realization of fidelity or authenticity [Wahrhaftigwerden] in the life of the individual through a pure surrender to a One.[76]

> It is simply the way of vital religion—inasmuch as it never concerns itself with something universal but rather always with one's own soul—to relate itself to facts in the experience of which one sees his own existence as connected with the all powerful One.[77]

Herrmann is himself very wary of this sort of generalizing:

> We should not ask how the revelation of God is experienced by persons but rather how we ourselves experience it. The way to faith is generally valid, for it awaits every person in the authenticity of his own inner life. But the experience in which faith is realized as pure surrender to a One is completely individual.[78]

Accordingly, his interpretation of religion is in turn related directly to the Christian experience from which it is in any case generalized:

We must develop religious judgments about the real out of the experience of the revelation of God. In so doing, we must remain aware of the fact that these thoughts can be valid for us as the expression of our own experience only if they do not deny their individual character. These thoughts can, then, relate us to other religious people only if they point to an event that is also experienced as revelation by them. Christian theology can become a power in its own right only in that it seeks to represent what it means for a person when the fact [Faktum] of the person of Jesus becomes revelation for him.[79]

The independence of theology is, then, said to be possible only if it is grounded in the individual's experience of revelation through the fact of the person of Jesus Christ. Thus Herrmann presents his own theological program as the preservation of Protestant autonomy against the heteronomy of the middle ages and the attempts of the Enlightenment to assault Christian faith and reduce it to subservience. That he explicitly identifies the alternative he is rejecting with Troeltsch is not surprising. Underlying their disagreement is the same systematic issue that Troeltsch formulates in the article on method in theology and explores in more detail in the essay on the significance of Jesus: whether the relationship between fact and faith is direct or indirect, immediate or mediated through the most comprehensive available historical context. Troeltsch's insistence that the historical sense of the post-Enlightenment West requires the integration of isolated events into more inclusive contexts does preclude Herrmann's grounding of the independence of theology in the direct connection between the personal experience of the believer and the God revealed in the inner life of Jesus. For Troeltsch as much as for Herrmann the issue is, however, still that of the relationship of faith to fact. Just as he does not in his Christological analysis, with its emphasis on the centrality of community and cult, reduce religious commitment to factual judgment, so Troeltsch also does not collapse dogmatics into historical study.

Troeltsch summarizes his position on this question of the relationship of dogmatics to historical study in an article published a year after Herrmann's essay. The article is a survey of theology during the second half of the nineteenth century. In it Troeltsch focuses on what he sees as the lamentable fact that historical and dogmatic studies, which both Schleiermacher and Ritschl attempted to unite, have increasingly gone separate ways. He then concludes his essay with a brief discussion of implications to be drawn from this situation for the further development of theology. His formulation of the problem is remarkably similar to Herrmann's analysis in that it too both stresses the need for untrammelled historical research and rejects the attempt to claim objective or theoretically demonstrable knowledge on behalf of dogmatics:

Every history is bound to general historical methods; and the theological pseudo-history, which construes things here according to rules and assumptions different from those that obtain in non-Christian studies, is forever condemned through its endless evasions and untruths. On the other hand, every conceivable dogmatics must take into account the idiosyncrasy [Eigenart] of religious discernment. Accordingly, it must renounce the goal of scientifically valid knowledge and both use and continue the powers of the tradition. The relationship of these two, the possibility that historical study and dogmatics coexist constructively, that is the vital question.[80]

Despite the similarities in formulation, the difference between this position and Herrmann's analysis is epitomized in Troeltsch's concluding emphasis on constructive interaction. Herrmann distinguishes religion and the academic disciplines so as to assert the independence of theology; Troeltsch similarly distinguishes dogmatics and historical studies—but only so as to urge their cooperation in the religious and theological task they share. His metaphor for this common effort is that of two branches with a common trunk. That common trunk is in Troeltsch's judgment certain to furnish a shared historical grounding based on studies of uncompromised integrity. But its core cannot be constituted through historical research as such:

The main question as to the validity of Christianity itself is no purely historical one. Instead it is a question for the philosophy of history or the philosophy of religion—a question which can be conceived in a disciplined intellectual sense only through a general theory of religion including philosophical and historical theory of its developmental stages.[81]

This approach, Troeltsch argues, avoids the alternative of merely arbitrary judgment and instead provides a foundation not only for dogmatics but also for ethics and church history, a foundation grounded in "comparative appraisal that proceeds from a consideration of the whole of historical life in so far as it is accessible to us."[82]

To this descriptive, comparative, evaluative, and constructive task, Troeltsch dedicated virtually all of his work at least from the long essay on "The Independence of Religion" (1895-1896) through *The Absoluteness of Christianity and the History of Religions* (1902) and *The Social Teachings of the Christian Churches* (1912) to *Historicism and its Problems* (1922) and the essays written just before his death and published posthumously as *Christian Thought: Its History and Application* (1923). Those writings testify to his seriousness in attempting to order the available data and also illustrate his willingness to revise his own always tentative conslusions. But even with the vicissitudes in Troeltsch's still developing position, the contrast between his and Herrmann's conception of the central theological task remains both systematic and significant. The contrast on this question of the relationship between theology and the historical disciplines in particular is, moreover, not without profound implications for Christian ethical and institutional life.

4.2 Ethics and the Essence of Christianity

Some of the ramifications of their disagreement over the relationship between theology and historical study are evident in Troeltsch's critical analysis of Herrmann's *Ethics* (first published in 1901 but also issued in repeatedly revised editions, the sixth and last of which appeared in 1921). Troeltsch praises Herrmann's book as "one of the most mature, most thoroughly thought-through, and intellectually most free works of contemporary theology." He also indicates considerable agreement with the "substantive content" that there is in his discussion of ethical issues.[83] But he at the same time registers his objection to the formalism that consistently characterizes Herrmann's approach—an objection that he (as if to reciprocate Herrmann's dual criticism of him) advances on historical as well as systematic grounds.

The historical criticism is directed at Herrmann's identification of Kantian ethics with the Christian moral ideal expressed in the New Testament. Troeltsch summarily rejects this identification or equation:

> Viewed strictly as a historical question, it is an extraordinary misapprehension of the meaning and spirit of the Gospel, and, given presently attained knowledge of the New Testament, is completely impossible.[84]

The question is not, however, simply a historical one, since, as Troeltsch also points out, "this equation . . . controls the whole conceptual structure" of Herrmann's position.[85] Consequently the problematical Kantian tendency to abstract from questions of objective or material good in favor of an exclusive emphasis on subjective motivation and formal autonomy is also both attributed to Jesus and applied in contemporary ethical analysis.

Troeltsch acknowledges that Herrmann's emphasis on inner disposition and autonomy rightly captures "a basic strain" in the Gospel accounts, especially of Jesus' opposition to Pharisaic legalism.[86] He also grants that Herrmann reintroduces at least some of the content of the Christian ethos indirectly—to take a central example, in maintaining that for Christianity individual goals are subordinate to those of the community.[87] Troeltsch's concern is, however, with the implications of Herrmann's procedure, even if "the genuineness and power of his reality sense" allow him to avoid some of the indicated outcomes himself.[88] Accordingly, Troeltsch pointedly formulates the line of argument that tacitly informs Herrmann's analysis:

> For Herrmann the great problem of the relationship between Christianity and culture is solved. The ascetic and world-indifferent character of Christianity is transformed into the rigor of an immanent autonomy; and cultural values are relegated to the status of mere preparations and materials for this autonomy.[89]

Troeltsch's criticism of this solution is elaborated in great detail but may be summarized concisely. It is that the distinction between formal disposition and material goods nominally resolves every conflict without addressing the substantive issues involved in the relationship between Christ and culture. As a result, the ethical good as it is imaged in the New Testament and elaborated in the history of the Christian tradition does not engage contemporary cultural life but rather through its exclusive emphasis on inner disposition in effect accepts whatever specific values and institutional patterns a particular historical context offers.[90]

Herrmann's interpretation of Christian ethics as centering on the interior disposition of the agent is, of course, integral to his consistent focus on the believer's direct relationship to God as revealed in the inner life of Jesus. In both cases, the contact or the continuity between the believer and Jesus is an almost completely formal one. Just as dependence on historical data about the life and teaching of Jesus is reduced to a bare minimum (if not eliminated totally) through Herrmann's contention that revelation is grounded exclusively on the inner life of Jesus, so the need for attention to such substantive ethical issues as the use of force or the legitimacy of economic planning is all but avoided through his allegedly exclusive grounding of the right on the interior disposition of the agent. This formalism in his analysis supports Herrmann's assertion of a direct relationship between Jesus and the individual believer despite the intervening centuries. Similarly, it allows Herrmann to interpret and to affirm development in the content of Christian moral reflection while at the same time insisting on an underlying identity. To note the most emphatic instance in his *Ethics,* Herrmann uses this formal/material distinction to justify a positive orientation to cultural life in this world in contrast to the enmity toward culture characteristic of the earliest Christian communities. What is crucial is to retain the authenticity of Jesus' disposition of unconditioned obedience to God rather than simply to repeat historically conditioned evaluations of competing material goods. "Thus," argues Herrmann, "we can follow him only if we go our own way."[91]

As Troeltsch notes in the course of his exposition of Herrmann's view, this approach is a reiteration of traditional Lutheran ethics, albeit in Kantian terminology and not without a spirit of rigor and activism that Herrmann himself shares with Calvinism. Like the Lutheran conception of two kingdoms, Herrmann's interpretation of Christian ethics joins unqualified trust in and subjection to the rule of God with an emphasis on performance of duty in the vocation to which the believer is called so that the necessary functions of the social order may be maintained. Indeed, the acceptance of worldly powers is even less qualified than in orthodox Lutheranism because Herrmann virtually eliminates the negative judgment implied in the traditional conception of the established social order as only a concession to human sin and therefore as finally incommensurable with the Christian ideal.[92]

Against Herrmann, Troeltsch contends that this Lutheran harmonizing solution is no more viable than the Roman Catholic appeal to natural law. Both positions are untenable because they are insufficiently historicized. The difficulties are transparent in the Roman Catholic commitment to an immutable order of nature that nonetheless requires authoritative ecclesiastical interpretation because of the effects of sin. But the Roman Catholic position does at least recognize that ethical issues involve conflict and compromise among competing material or objective goods—in contrast to Herrmann's location of transhistorical constancy in the formal identity of the autonomous disposition that all moral agents have in common. Troeltsch concurs with the Roman Catholic emphasis on mediating among conflicting goods while rejecting its appeal to an immutable natural law; consequently he maintains that Christian ethics must entail the constant effort to relate religious ideals that are themselves not exempt from development to the complex historical processes of a continuously changing secular life. This relationship can never be more than one of approximation and compromise in which Christianity attempts to shape culture and is at the same time accommodated to it. But the interaction is unavoidable and should not be obscured either through appeal to the material relationships specified in an allegedly unchanging natural law or through exhortations to a formal disposition that in effect accepts whatever order prevails.[93]

The Social Teachings of the Christian Churches is, of course, Troeltsch's detailed historical exploration of this enormously complex range of issues. In that work, he collects and orders voluminous data from the history of Christian thought and practice to illustrate his position over against the simpler, less thoroughly historicized, alternatives. On occasion Troeltsch's exposition directly echoes his criticism of the Ritschlians. In describing Jesus' preaching, for example, Troeltsch notes the completely unselfconscious references in the Synoptic accounts to heavenly rewards for the faithful—and contrasts this orientation to the artificial attempt "to construe the Gospel ethic as a purely subjective morality of disposition, as the demand for action in accordance with the dictates of the autonomous conscience alone."[94] But a more sustained analysis of the similarities and differences between his approach to the interaction of Christianity and culture and that of the older Ritschlians is provided in a series of essays that Troeltsch published in the *Christliche Welt* in 1903 with the collective title "What is the Meaning of 'Essence of Christianity'?"

The essays take the form of a commentary on Harnack's *The Essence of Christianity* (1900). Troeltsch observes that Harnack's lectures are "to a certain extent the symbolic book for the historicizing tendency in theology":

> In place of dogmatics appears the infinitely simpler, more effective, and more convincing historical portrayal of the Gospel and its further influence as the essence of Christianity.[95]

In Harnack's lectures Troeltsch is, then, considering those emphases in Ritschlianism that he himself finds most congenial—in short, its historical as opposed to dogmatic tendencies. Indeed, he argues that the very expression "Essence of Christianity" has its origins in "modern, critical, developmental, historical study." He grants that it can be and increasingly is appropriated for use in other contexts—even that of Roman Catholic dogmatics, for example, which in the past would have referred instead simply to "the faith of the church." But this frame of reference of historical study is the one to which Harnack appeals. It is also the one that Troeltsch himself takes to be the most illuminating. Accordingly, he analyzes the essence of Christianity as a strictly historical conception and in the process provides an appraisal of Harnack's line of argument on the basis of its own implied even if not always observed premises.[96]

In contrast to Harnack's emphasis on the self-evident simplicity and unilinear continuity of the "kernel" of Christianity in and through its varying "husks,"Troeltsch focuses attention on the multidimensionality of the tradition and on the active process of selection and criticism which is involved in any specification of its essence. There are multiple conceptions of the essence of Christianity, each of which is "not merely an abstraction from appearances, but also at the same time a criticism of the appearances."[97] That the essence of Christianity is a critical principle and not simply the product of description forces consideration of the question of criteria for adjudicating among claimants for the title and also underscores the subjective component in any final decision. But it is, Troeltsch argues, surely better to address this complex of questions directly than to engage in the self-delusion that objective and immutable norms are available. Otherwise the values of the historian or of a more or less provincial strain in the tradition may assume an authority that derives from unjustified pretensions to an inclusive and therefore exclusive representation of the tradition as a whole.[98]

The danger of uncritically totalizing a single dimension of the tradition is especially pronounced with respect to its origins. Just as Harnack refers to the final subjectivism in judgments as to the truth of the traditions a historian describes, he also acknowledges the need to survey the influence that Jesus exerted to see what further truth it reveals about his personality and teachings.[99] But here again Troeltsch centers his analysis on what is peripheral for Harnack. Troeltsch concurs with Harnack that precisely for a historical approach, the origins of a tradition unavoidably attain a special prominence. He insists, however, that the further development of the tradition is also integral to its essence not only because the origin itself is illumined through its historical elaboration but also because "new elements" are taken up into an "evolving spiritual principle." A straightforward recognition of this fact liberates both the historian and the believer from those "after-effects" of Protestant Biblicism which continue the attempt to locate everything of value in Christianity within the New Testament. At the same time, this affirmation of novelty as legitimate counters the tendency to seek uncritical support for cherished contemporary values through appeal to the authority of allegedly unchanging original truths.[100]

Troeltsch maintains that any conception of the essence of Christianity which seeks to do justice to the variety of the tradition not only in its origins but also in its development cannot in any sense be "a simple concept, like being a child of God, spiritual or personalistic religion, faith in God as father or the like." Instead the specification of the essence must include tensions and even contradictions within it. In typically Troeltschian fashion, he offers multiple formulations of the polarities or dualisms to which every conception of the essence of Christianity must do justice. But the governing tension is between the eschatological preaching of Jesus with its total commitment to the transhistorical kingdom of God on the one hand and the unavoidable accommodations to and appropriations of culture in the Christian tradition on the other. Both thrusts are integral to the essence of Christianity. To emphasize this complementarity, Troeltsch refers critically to the organic metaphor frequently used to express appreciation for development in traditions—in Alfred Loisy's *The Gospel and the Church* (1902), to note one example that Troeltsch considered very illuminating. In the terms of this metaphor, Troeltsch maintains that the essence of Christianity cannot be imaged simply as the germination of a bud. Troeltsch himself identifies the germ or bud with the preaching of Jesus and argues that it has a definite authority over against every adaptation of Christianity to culture. But the essence of Christianity is not reducible to the unfolding of what is originally present. Instead the dynamic tension between the two poles, between the transcendent and the immanent orientations within Christianity, is both definitive of its essence and indispensable to its vitality and fruitfulness. [101]

The difference between their positions is illustrated in Troeltsch's response to a criticism Harnack registers in a review of the *Social Teachings of the Christian Churches*. Harnack objects to the emphatic subordination of love for the neighbor to love of God in Troeltsch's account of Jesus' preaching. [102] In a footnote added to his essay "Fundamental Problems of Ethics . . . ," Troeltsch refers to this criticism and comments that Harnack like Herrmann interprets the command to love the neighbor "in a more Christian-socialist sense." [103] Troeltsch does not even reply directly to the criticism because his response is implied in his position as a whole. For him there is no need to ground contemporary commitments to Christian social reform directly in the preaching of Jesus. Instead, Jesus remains the proclaimer of a transcendent liberation that forever stands in tension with every immanent ethical program. The need for such programs is integral to the very essence of Christianity; but no specific set of prescriptions can be absolutized as the enduring expression of that essence. [104]

5 Another Look at Culture-Protestantism

In the foregoing discussion of method, of Christology, and of ethics, I have argued that there are distinctions within what is usually referred to as theological liberalism—distinctions that represent not simply disagreements as to emphasis but rather systematically differentiable positions. Insofar as that argument is persuasive, it requires a reviewing of the systematic issues and the historical questions to which the name "Culture-Protestantism" calls attention. Indeed, the central thesis which such a review must elaborate is already evident. This thesis is that if the designation is to be of any use at all, its reference must be differentiated so as to indicate the multiple positions which it encompasses. Unless the term is abandoned, which seems unlikely at least in the German-speaking world, there must, in short, be a specification of the systematically significant variations in Culture-Protestantism.

5.1 Variations in Culture-Protestantism

The differentation in the reference of the term "Culture-Protestantism" that follows most directly from the foregoing discussion is, of course, the one implied in the contrast between the Ritschlians and the history of religions school, with the thought of Kaftan, Herrmann, and Harnack as representative of the most influential versions of the former and Troeltsch's position as the most systematic formulation of the latter. It is, however, illuminating to view his successors in relation to Ritschl's own approach as a distinct position from which they distance themselves in different (though not simply opposite) directions.

Both the resources for shaping culture and the susceptibility to being conformed to it are evident in Ritschl's rejection of the conceptions of natural law and natural religion. The resources for active and constructive influence of Christianity on culture are striking. Through his insistent grounding of Christianity on revelation rather than on so-called natural knowledge, Ritschl asserts the independence of theology over against not only the natural sciences but also philosophy. This independent theology is, moreover, both social and dynamic inasmuch as its authority is said to derive from the New Testament revelation of a fully personal God who establishes the divine rule or kingdom as the corporate purpose and goal of the world. Consistent with this affirmation of development is Ritschl's exuberant embrace of the historical over against the natural. But this sharp contrast between the natural and the historical is at the same time a source for the susceptibility to uncritical conformism in his position because the appeal to culture as opposed to nature

43

in effect legitimates the aspirations of one definite ethos over against the alternatives challenging it.

An address that Ritschl delivered two years before his death illustrates the connections forcefully. In this speech he offers his analysis of the recent political fact that Roman Catholic centrist elements, liberals, and social democrats had formed a coalition. His concern is to alert those "citizens interested in stability and security" to the historical grounding for this cooperation so as to counter the illusion that it constitutes only a coincidental and passing rather than a recurrent danger.[105] After rehearsing the teachings of Aquinas, Cardinal Robert Bellarmin, and Hugo Grotius, Ritschl offers his own summary:

> The Roman Catholic, the socialist, and the specifically liberal view of the state have their common grounding in the incorrect setting over against each other of the imaginary law of nature and historical law.[106]

The result of this erroneous conceptualization is that natural law may be invoked against historically established authority—in contrast to even the libertarian strain in the Lutheran heritage, which still does not oppose "the conservative task of the historically understood state."[107] He then concludes his address with congratulations to those engaged in historical study at the University of Göttingen (including, of course, a member of the theological faculty named Ritschl) for their diligence in demonstrating that both natural law and natural religion are fictions, since all law and all religion are "positive and concrete."[108]

This speech expresses very vividly the extent to which established institutions and existing interest were imbued with an inherent legitimacy in Ritschl's perspective. This tendency in his theology is, of course, the one that is emphasized in Niebuhr's *Christ and Culture* and Barth's chapter on Ritschl in *Protestant Theology in the Nineteenth Century*. It is tempting simply to observe that Ritschl is a product of his time and place and to leave it at that: his Prussian origins, his unwavering support for Bismark, and his uncritically bourgeois values conspired with the Lutheran conceptions of fidelity to one's vocation and patient acceptance of one's station in life to subvert the resources his theology had for genuine engagement between Christianity and culture. The accuracy of this observation should not, however, obscure the systematic issue which Ritschl's position serves to focus for his successors. He is after all right in his assertion that natural law and natural religion are generalized human constructs, the only instances of which are particular historical traditions—even if his use of that insight to counter the critical power of such conceptions is reprehensible. And not only the Ritschlians but also Troeltsch agree with him that to continue inherited uses of the conceptions of natural religion and natural law is anachronistic. The question is, therefore, whether they are more successful than he is in referring to or conceiving that which transcends existing interests and established institutions.

With respect to Kaftan, Herrmann, and Harnack, the answer to this question is unambiguously negative. Kaftan combined a social conservatism not unlike Ritschl's with his individualistic mysticism and increasingly influential positions in the anything but liberal Prussian church hierarchy. Herrmann and Harnack were, to be sure, somewhat less conservative than Ritschl both theologically and politically. But the direction of their movement from his systematic position nonetheless compromised what potential there is in Ritschl's thought for a dynamic and social theology. Like Ritschl, they sought to invoke the authority of revelation for cherished contemporary values. But in part because they retained only very little of Ritschl's residual Biblicism, they increasingly individualized and privatized the commitments they commended as grounded in revelation—a process of individualization and privatization that is epitomized in Herrmann's *Ethics* and Harnack's *The Essence of Christianity*. The rule of God was, in short, more and more identified with the faith of the infinitely valuable personal soul or with the purity of the agent's disposition rather than as a public community participating in and working to realize the divine goal or purpose for the world.

The movement from Ritschl to the Ritschlians reflected and in turn influenced pervasive cultural patterns of the era. Viewed in the context of intellectual history from the beginning of the nineteenth to the middle of the twentieth centuries, this movement within a very definite theological tradition parallels and participates in the enormously varied developments that may be schematized as a shift from idealism to existentialism—with Ritschl still very much under the influence of the former and especially Herrmann increasingly representative of the latter. Both the theological and the more inclusive cultural developments were, of course, also interrelated with the social history of the period. If Ritschl expressed the self-confidence not only of an ascendant bourgeoisie but also of a newly unified and increasingly powerful German state that was in the still relatively early stages of unprecedentedly rapid industrialization and expansion in population, then Kaftan, Harnack, and Herrmann came to reflect misgivings as to the unambiguous beneficence of this series of developments, misgivings not unrelated to the political uncertainty following the unexpected accession to the throne of a virtually unknown and very young Kaiser in 1888 and the removal of Bismark from the government in 1890.

In terms of the interface between religion and society, the forces interacting in this complex historical situation are illustrated in an institution organized in 1890, the Evangelisch-soziale Kongress. Even its founding is characteristic for the period in that it exemplifies the intimate interdependence of the church, including activities in social service or social action, and the empire. In January 1890 the Reichstag in effect acknowledged the defeat of the more than decade old attempt to outlaw the social democratic party and declined to extend the legal ban on its activity. To meet the challenge which the now legalized social democrats posed, the Kaiser issued two directives in February 1890. The directives supported the principle of governmental protection for worker interests and called for international cooperation in setting industrial standards that meet the legitimate needs and aspirations of labor. Then in April 1890 the central administration of the Protestant state church (Oberkirchenrat) officially urged its ministers to participate in "the formation of workers' associations" and to appear at open meetings called for the purpose so as "to destroy the prejudices of workers" against the clergy.[109] At the same time, on the initiative of the court preacher Adolf Stoecker, the Evangelisch-sociale Kongress was organized as a forum for relating Protestantism to the pressing and increasingly evident social problems of workers in particular. The Kongress held its first meeting in May 1890.

From its inception the Evangelisch-soziale Kongress had a powerful conservative wing under Stoecker's leadership which wanted to alleviate the distress of workers so as to save them from socialism and for throne and altar. But it also included increasing numbers of younger and more liberal members who coalesced around Friedrich Naumann, even if they did not all share his conviction as to the need for working with the social democrats. It did not take long for both Stoecker and the church hierarchy to become disenchanted with the increasingly active support for labor among those in this liberal faction. In 1896 Stoecker and others associated closely with him withdrew from the Kongress to organize a more cohesively church-centered rival association, the Freie kirchlich-soziale Konferenz. And in December 1895, the central administration of the Protestant state church issued a remarkable statement designed to communicate the lessons learned since its 1890 exhortation to clergy concerning the desirability of their participation in worker associations. The new statement speaks of the need for "constrictions" in its earlier mandate, since too many clergy have shown themselves unable to master their passion for taking sides and have thus "compromised their clerical office" by aligning themselves with "a single class of the population."[110] In contrast to this unseemly behavior, the directive formulates the church's proper role:

> The church's influence on external areas can and may never be a direct one, but only an indirect one that is inwardly fruitful.[111]

The statement then notes that the "foundations of our common being" are "fear of God, fidelity to the king, and love for the neighbor." Accordingly, the clergy are exhorted to perform their pastoral duties faithfully, to remind those with earthly goods that their stewardship should include charitable acts, and to impress on the poor the value of honest work and frugality and the sinfulness of envy. Finally, the directive concludes with the hope that clergy will take corrective action themselves so that the hierarchy will not have to employ its disciplinary powers.[112]

This statement represents the extreme of official reaction against direct Christian involvement in social struggles and political action. As such, it certainly cannot be identified with the views of the Ritschlians. The shift in position between the 1890 and the 1895 directives is, however, an admittedly exaggerated image of developments within the Evangelisch-soziale Kongress itself. And in those developments, prominent Ritschlians (Kaftan, Herrmann, and Harnack among others) did participate. As Manfred Schick documents in his analysis of the published stenographic transcripts of the annual meetings of the Kongress, there was in the course of the years an increasing emphasis on what he terms "the ideal of personality" and a correlative decrease in references to the kingdom of God.[113] And impetus for movement in this direction came repeatedly from the Ritschlians.

Already in the second annual meeting of 1891, Herrmann gave a lecture which programmatically divorces economic and religious considerations. He is consistent in maintaining that opposition to socialism can be grounded theologically no more than support for it.[114] But he also states that the so-called "social question" is in the last analysis "the consciousness of humanity as to the distress intrinsic to its history." It is accordingly no more soluble than what for human reason is the contradiction between a lawful world of nature and affirmation of an all-powerful and loving God. From this parallel, Herrmann indicates the conclusion applicable not only to the divide between theology and the sciences but also to the disjunction between religion and social tensions:

> The point is not to overcome that contradiction, but rather to understand it, to become personally [innerlich] finished with it.[115]

Another illustration of the role of the Ritschlians in the Kongress is Kaftan's address at the 1893 annual meeting. Like Herrmann, Kaftan maintains that "Christian religion and economic life are as such separate spheres"—the former concerned with "eternal life in God" and the latter with "satisfaction of temporal needs."[116] But he then relates the two spheres through attention to the Christian affirmation that ethical activity is the necessary way to the goal of eternal life. This ethical life is social and is summed up in the command of love. The "necessary presupposition of all ethical life" is, however, "personal life and human consciousness of personhood."[117] Accordingly, Christian duty requires "both the defense of the essential foundations of the established economic order against revolutionary impulses and incisive demands with reference to its reformation." Among the foundations of the established order, he specifies private property and social stratification according to professions as especially supportive of personal freedom, independence, and "the exalted spiritual atmosphere" necessary for the nurture of "Protestant Christianity, with its high spiritual and ethical demands on the individual." And to exemplify the need for reform, he protests eloquently against all practices which reduce the person to a mere means:

> The spiritual-ethical personality may never be sacrificed to the economic growth of the whole.[118]

The respondent to Kaftan's address was Naumann. In his response, he takes exception to the governing role that the conception of personality plays in Kaftan's approach. He insists that the Gospel has direct social relevance apart from every consideration of personal ethical worth:

> That earth should be relieved of all pain and suffering is for Christ not first mediated through the dialectical thought of personal ethical worth. Rather, it is immediate religion to overcome suffering wherever it confronts one.[119]

Naumann argues that it is this dimension of the Gospel that social democracy, which he designates as "the first great Protestant heresy," is forcing established Christianity to face.[120] Later in the discussion, Harnack then tries to integrate both viewpoints, though he offers his remarks as a criticism of Naumann:

> Kaftan derived everything that we as Christians must demand with reference to the economic order essentially from the concept of the value of the human soul; in contrast, Naumann . . . saw the decisive motif in social formation. . . . I find that one cannot separate the two points of view.

His own immediately following formulation of the double perspective is, however, revealing in the priority it accords to the individual:

> One cannot form a brotherhood unless one recognizes personality in the full power which it should express. Conversely, when one holds to personality as the Christian should acknowledge it—that is, as the immortal soul—then the duty of brotherhood and charity also obtains.[121]

That Harnack and Kaftan as well as Herrmann were strongly individualistic in their theologies scarely requires detailed documentation. It is, however, worth noting the extent to which their writings express a tendency also evident, in part through their influence, in even an organization like the Evangelisch-soziale Kongress. Despite its intention to address pressing societal issues, the Kongress, in short, illustrates the rapid atrophying of the social and dynamic thrust at least potentially present in a theological system like that of Ritschl. Thus Culture-Protestantism assumes a different form for the older Ritschlians than for Ritschl himself. Whereas Ritschl's theology evidences impressive resources for critical engagement with culture, his optimism and confidence in historical developments already in process precluded the realization of what potential there is. In contrast, the older Ritschlians express interest in addressing societal issues that are increasingly unavoidable. At the same time, however, they revise Ritschl's position so as to eliminate precisely those emphases which provide points of contact with concrete historical problems.

Even Naumann was not exempt from the development illustrated in the movement from Ritschl to the Ritschlians and in the shifting orientation of the Evangelisch-soziale Kongress. From his employment as a pastor and social worker both in a mining community and in Frankfurt, Naumann was intensely interested in articulating a social theology. Until the mid 1890s, he wrote and lectured extensively on the need for Christian socialism, on the value of Marxist analysis and socialist organization, on the challenges and opportunities of industrialism for Christianity. By the turn of the century he was, however, himself very dubious about his earlier Marxist-inspired and Ritschl-influenced program.

In his monograph, *Friedrich Naumann's Theological Recantation,* Hermann Timm portrays this change forcefully—even if he at times overstates his case for dramatic effect. [122] In part because of a trip to Palestine and in part because of the findings of New Testament research, Naumann became convinced that no positive social program could be grounded in the teaching and ministry of Jesus. Through his own experience combined with the influence of Max Weber, he became increasingly convinced that only a state socialism for which church efforts were all but irrelevant could address the needs of an industrial society. Accordingly, his own religious orientation became increasingly personal and individualistic. In his popular *Letters on Religion* (issued in repeated editions, the first of which appeared in 1903), for example, he notes that the difficulties of relating Jesus' ministry and teachings to contemporary life are much greater than he had once thought; and he even commends Luther for the clarity with which he "separated spiritual and worldly things."[123] As for the parallels between his own development and that of the Evangelisch-soziale Kongress, Naumann himself alludes to them in his response to a paper at the 1911 annual meeting. He notes that if the Kongress were founded again then, it would have to be named not "evangelisch-sozial" but rather "protestantisch-ideal" to record the extent to which the interests of the organization had shifted from the social relevance of the Gospel to a Reformation and Kantian preoccupation with "the cultivation of the individual, the personality." And the same Naumann who criticized Kaftan in 1893 adds: "I am not saying whether rightly or wrongly; rather I am only describing what I see."[124]

That leaves Troeltsch.

Like the older Ritschlians, Troeltsch distances himself from Ritschl's position. Unlike them, he does not, however, move in an ever more consistently individualistic Lutheran and Kantian direction. An admittedly arbitrary emblem of the difference is Schick's passing reference to one of the few exceptions to his generalization that the concept of the kingdom of God became far less prominent in the deliberations of the Evangelisch-soziale Kongress over the years. The exception he notes is Troeltsch's concluding remarks following the discussion of his address at the 1904 meeting of the Kongress. In those remarks Troeltsch observes that the only unified intentionality in Christian ethics is expressed in the entreaty "Thy Kingdom come."[125] Troeltsch is not proposing a return to Ritschl's interpretation of Jesus as the self-conscious founder of an ethical commonwealth. This address and the accompanying discussion, even if taken by themselves, amply illustrate his profound differences with Ritschl—differences evident in his positive references to natural orders, in his emphasis on Jesus' otherworldliness, in his rejection of the identification between early Christian ethics and a formally unified will in the Kantian sense, and in his disparaging remarks about the Lutheran as compared to the Roman Catholic and Reformed traditions.[126] But despite all such differences, Troeltsch shares Ritschl's concern with concrete historical developments and hence accords social and cultural processes a centrality in theology and ethics that stands in contrast to the efforts the Ritschlians direct toward establishing formal and atemporal points of contact between Jesus and Christians of every era.

In his lecture to the Evangelisch-soziale Kongress, Troeltsch addresses what he sees as the need to develop a Christian political ethic for the contemporary situation. He is persuaded that it is possible to approach this task more self-consciously than in the past because the double awareness of the radically eschatological character of the New Testament and of the enormously diverse development of Christian theological and ethical commitments frees contemporary Christians from either attempting to derive all ethical principles from the Bible or uncritically absolutizing such particular past borrowings as the individualistic natural law of late antiquity.[127] Troeltsch's own formulation of a contemporary Christian political ethic calls for a combination of two central strains throughout the tradition, one of them expressed in "revolutionary and democratic tendencies," the other in "aristocratic and conservative ones." The two thrusts in Christianity are "the thought of the absolute value of the personality" and "the thought of submission to God's naturally ordered world." The political ethic Troeltsch envisions must reintegrate these two central Christian commitments while at the same time purging them of their respective accretions—"in the one case natural law, with its natural equality of human beings and human purposes, and in the other case the divinization of past power relationships, with its obsessive clutching to established possessions, its eternalizing of the *status quo,* its opposition to advances and reforms."[128]

Troeltsch argues that the intention of a Christian ethic cannot be to elaborate its own political program. Instead the Christian and the church must engage in a constant "evaluating and influencing of the parties and programs that emerge from the natural process of political development."[129] As his formulation of a contemporary political ethic indicates, the result of Troeltsch's own appraisal of the parties and programs of the time is support for a liberalism that demands reform in opposition not only to the conservatives of the right and middle but also to egalitarian socialism on the left. Troeltsch himself resisted direct participation in politics, though when he became convinced that the seriousness of the situation demanded involvement in the last years of the war and its aftermath, he also acted from this liberal frame of reference, first in helping to organize an association opposed to German annexationist policies and then as an elected representative of the German Democratic Party after the war.[130]

In Troeltsch's view, intimate interconnections between the in the first instance personal concerns of Christianity on the one hand and social and cultural forces on the other are, then, not only unavoidable but also to be affirmed. This position may with some justice be termed "Culture-Protestantism." It is, however, a form of Culture-Protestantism different from those of Ritschl and the Ritschlians. It is pluralistic and critical in contrast to Ritschl's tendency toward sanguine affirmation of an allegedly unified line of development. And it is concerned with the compromises and approximations involved in all concrete attempts to ethicize the social order in contrast to the formalistic and individualistic tendencies of the older Ritschlians that in effect legitimate existing historical patterns with the authority of the ideal. Efforts at overcoming deficiencies in the alternative approaches of course entail their own dangers. The attempt to do justice to pluralism while at the same time aspiring to inclusiveness not only holds the promise of relating Christianity to its comprehensive historical context but also threatens to dissolve this one tradition into a bewildering array of internal differentiations and external correlations. Similarly, an awareness of the inherent complexity and impurity of efforts to relate Christianity to culture counters formalistic and individualistic simplifications only at the risk that acknowledgement of the relativity of the historical norms employed in concrete decisions may be misconstrued as unqualified relativism. But—to personalize the issue—Troeltsch preferred this set of dangers as represented in a figure like Naumann, even the Naumann of *Letters on Religion,* to the deficiencies he saw in Herrmann's position. Thus he comments about Naumann that "his views stem from the most genuine and mature experience" and contrasts that to "the impression one gets with Herrmann, as with so many works in theological ethics, of paper constructions completely removed from the world."[131] Troeltsch preferred, in short, to err in the direction of immersion in the world rather than to risk abstraction from it.

5.2   Culture-Protestantism: From Indictment to Conviction

If allowance is made for its multiple variations through a sufficiently encompassing and nuanced use of the term, the indictment of turn-of-the-century theological liberalism as Culture-Protestantism is, then, sustained. Ritschl, the Ritschlians, the history of religions school, and such free spirits as Naumann and Rade whose guilt is by association with all three theological generations are convicted as charged. That there are differences in their versions of Culture-Protestantism does not alter the fact that they are all still Culture-Protestants.

The sweeping character of this verdict serves to focus the question of whether or not anyone is excluded from the judgment that is pronounced. In particular attention is attracted to the witnesses for the prosecution. There is Barth's portrayal of Christoph Blumhardt as the representative of the future over against the past of Naumann. There is also Barth's defense of dialectical theology and attack against its detractors in his exchanges with Harnack in the *Christliche Welt.* And then there are the appraisals that Barth and Friedrich Gogarten offer of the positions of their teachers, Herrmann and Troeltsch respectively. The question is whether or not their testimony against the accused clarifies a viable alternative to Culture-Protestantism.

In a series of articles in the first volumes of the journal that served as an early organ for dialectical theology, *Zwischen den Zeiten,* Gogarten directs his sustained attack against what he considers the illusions of culture-idealism. The central issue is precisely the one that Troeltsch focuses in his essay on historical and dogmatic method:

> And the decision which these reflections are intended to specify unambiguously is this: whether one wants to see and conceive of this one finite appearance [the revelation of God in Christ] from the perspective of the infinite context of what in general occurs or whether one wants to let this one finite appearance be the beginning, middle, and end of one's own being and doing and thinking and the beginning, middle, and end of earth and heaven.[132]

The difference between Gogarten and Troeltsch is thus epitomized in their formulating the same systematic contrast—and then taking the opposite sides as self-evidently the right ones.

Like Troeltsch in the years just after the war, Gogarten stresses "the unheard of distress of this time, its ghastly confusion and its collapse that gathers momentum from day to day."[133] But he explicitly rejects the course that Troeltsch pursues with almost driven persistence in his massive *Historicism and its Problems* (1922), in the planned second volume of this work that he died before completing, and in such popular lectures/essays as "The Significance of History for the Weltanschauung" (1918) and *German Bildung* (1919). Against this attempt of Troeltsch and others to work toward a critical reappropriation, a new and more viable synthesis, of values from Christianity and other Western traditions, Gogarten has a summary judgment which he repeats as a refrain: "The world is at the end of its wisdom and its culture."[134] "To undertake a building anew of our destroyed world" as do those who commend reforms in education and cultural forms is in the end a "betrayal" and a "delusion" because it debases the human precisely through "human self-glorification" or "self-divinization."[135] In proposing his alternative to all such efforts, Gogarten at the same time offers his uncompromisingly negative judgment on them:

> What we should do is not to strive to improve the world in this or that way. Rather we should try to maintain the world as it is so that the one dreadful world which is always

threatened by the evil one does not destroy itself. Today it is doing that. And we help
with this devilish self-destruction if we try to improve the world through our actions—if
we, that is, work for a new culture in the sense in which that is understood today.
Through such efforts we serve the cunning of the evil one, even if we do it with the best of
intentions.[136]

Against Troeltsch, Gogarten can register an unqualified judgment insofar
as he reverses his teacher's line of argument and espouses dogmatic over
against historical method in theology. But Herrmann focuses on the fact of
Jesus Christ as such rather than beginning with the most comprehensive
historical context available. Consequently the same axis of differentiation
does not serve to distinguish dialectical theology from his position. Perhaps
this common ground between them over against Troeltsch accounts for the
very much less severe judgment that Barth pronounces on his teacher.

In any case, Barth has as much praise as blame in his assessment. Indeed,
Barth presents his analysis as an attempt to show that if Herrmann had only
been more consistent, he would have been a dialectical theologian himself.
Hence Barth commends Herrmann for his insistence that Christian truth must
be grounded in itself rather than through appeals to extrinsic authorities.[137]
But he then invokes this principle which Herrmann espouses in order to
criticize his claims for a general theory of religion that focuses on the self's
attainment of authenticity. More consistent, Barth maintains, would be to
insist on the objectivity of the revelation of God and its absolute priority to
every so-called personal experience.[138] Similarly, Barth interprets Herrmann's
focus on the inner life of Jesus as his attempt to stress the historically
indisputable reality of revelation.[139] But since there is no person of Jesus apart
from the Logos, Barth contends that Herrmann in fact takes his point of
departure from the exalted Christ:

The fact with which he began was, then,—one must consciously overrule his protest at
this point—the resurrected, the exalted Christ.[140]

As a result, Herrmann's theology is said to include unrealized potential for
exploding the correlation of subjectivity and objectivity in revelation and for
proclaiming in its place "the single act of the regal Christ ruling in the word
through the spirit in his church."[141]

Here Barth echoes the themes of his exchanges with Harnack and his
celebration of Blumhardt in contrast to Naumann. But he himself presents
this position as a radicalization of Herrmann's theology. As he puts it in the
opening paragraph of this essay:

The fact of an actual conversion away from Herrmann I could never have admitted to
myself—and could not to this day.[142]

Similarly, Gogarten's criticism of Troeltsch, with its echoes of the essay on
dogmatic and historical method, suggests the common ground between

dialectical theology just after the war and those Ritschlians who like
Herrmann and Kaftan opposed the history of religions school. There are, of
course, also systematic differences that result precisely from the radicalization
to which Barth calls attention. But those differences serve only to accentuate
even more the isolation of revelation from every available historical context.
Consequently, the position of dialectical theology also, and even more
extremely, evidences the tendency to formalism and abstraction that
Troeltsch criticizes in Herrmann when he calls for attention to the need for
approximation and compromise in adjudicating among concrete and
substantive alternatives. The issue is, in short, posed most systematically and
consistently between Barth and Troeltsch.

The contrast between Barth and Troeltsch emerges dramatically against
the background of developments in this tradition of theology from Ritschl on.
Ritschl himself appropriated the Kantian distinction between reason in its
theoretical and practical employments in order to separate cultural life in
general and theology and ethics in particular from the realm of nature and the
methods employed in the natural sciences. The older Ritschlians then
progressively narrowed the grounding of their theologies from the relatively
broad and somewhat uncritical claims that Ritschl himself had made for the
historical foundations of his work. The sharpest focus of all was that of
Herrmann, with his constant references to the fact of the person or the inner
life of Jesus. Over against this tendency toward increasingly drastic selections
within the cultural realm, Troeltsch moved toward a more and more inclusive
position for which the category of the historical overcame even the distinction
between nature and culture. Hence the contrast with Barth is total. Whereas
Troeltsch attempted to relate his theology integrally to historical processes
that encompass all of nature and culture, Barth insisted adamantly that the
revelation of God absolutely, infinitely, totally transcends the whole of the
cultural as well as the natural world.

This essay is not the forum for a detailed evaluation of the alternative that
Barth represents. It is, however, worth noting two striking metaphors with
which Harnack ends his postscript to the series of exchanges he has with Barth
in the *Christliche Welt*. Harnack depicts Barth's attempt to speak of a purely
objective revelation that even in its influence or efficacy allegedly excludes
human reception and understanding as leading "across an invisible ridge
between absolute religious scepticism and naive Biblicism." And he then asks:

> If he who apprehends Christian faith in this way and no other manages to retain his
> footing on this his glacial bridge, is there still room on it even only for his children and
> friends?[143]

I for one am convinced that historical developments both within and outside
theology since the 1920s as well as systematic considerations especially in
epistemology require a negative answer to Harnack's question.[144] There is, in

short, no tenable alternative to one or another variation of Culture-Protestantism since there is no theological standpoint divorced from human culture. Accordingly, a comparative and critical version of Culture-Protestantism and its equivalents in other traditions—a position like the one that Troeltsch's approach represents—is a matter of conviction also in the positive rather than only in the negative sense of the word.

Notes

[1] *Geschichte der neueren evangelischen Theologie,* vol. 5 (Gütersloh: C. Bertelsmann, 1954), p. 156. I hesitate to quote Hirsch because his well-known Nazi affiliations during the Third Reich cannot but call into question his authority to analyze the relationship between Christianity and culture. In spite of his reprehensible political associations, Hirsch's history of post-Enlightenment Protestant thought is, however, undeniably perceptive and continues to be very influential. As the fact that he was a devoted admirer of Kierkegaard should suggest, it is, moreover, a highly dubious exercise in oversimplification to trace Hirsch's political views directly to his limited defense of Culture-Protestantism.

[2] *Christ and Culture* (New York: Harper and Row—Torchbooks, 1956), p. 84. I have corrected a typographical error ("is is" to "it is") in the second quoted sentence. I have also omitted a footnote number; the footnote refers to Karl Barth as the person who Niebuhr thinks invented the term "Culture-Protestantism." In the section of Barth's *Protestantische Theologie im 19. Jahrhundert* to which Niebuhr refers, the term itself is not, however, used. Despite considerable effort, I have not been able to locate an instance of the term that does not already presuppose a general awareness of its meaning. Unselfconscious use of the name derives in part from the frequency in German of such terms as "culture-state," "culture-ideal" and so on. It no doubt also reflects origins as the informal characterization for an opposed position. But I have not been able to find definite evidence as to the "invention" of the term.

[3] *Christ and Culture,* pp. 101-2. In view of the prominence of the thought of Ernst Troeltsch in the line of argument which I am advancing, it should be noted that Niebuhr does not include him among those identified as illustrating the cultural Protestantism of the nineteenth century. See *Christ and Culture,* pp. 83-101 and 181-83.

[4] This lecture was delivered to the Goethegesellschaft Hannover in January 1957. It is reprinted in Barth, *Die protestantische Theologie im 19. Jahrhundert* (Hamburg: Siebenstern Taschenbuch, 1975), vol. 2. pp. 572-90. The quoted passage is from pp. 574-75.

[5] The appeal and the names of the signers are reproduced in G. F. Nicolai, *Die Biologie des Krieges, erster Band* (Zürich: Art. Institut Orell Füssli, 1919), pp. 7-10.

[6] *The Epistle to the Romans,* E. C. Hoskyns, trans. (Oxford: University Press, 1933), p. 7 / *Der Römerbrief* (München: Chr. Kaiser, 1924), p. XI.

[7] The essays on Naumann and Blumhardt appeared in 1919 both in the *Neuer Freier Aargauer,* numbers 204 and 205, and in *Der Christliche Demokrat* (later named *Das Neue Werk*), numbers 25 and 28. They are more readily accessible in *Anfänge der dialektischen Theologie,* J. Moltmann, ed. (München: Chr. Kaiser, 1962), pp. 37-49. The quoted passages are from pp. 43 and 49. The

essays are also available in English translation: "Past and Future: Friedrich Naumann and Christoph Blumhardt," K. R. Crim, trans. in *The Beginnings of Dialectical Theology,* J. M. Robinson, ed. (Richmond: John Knox Press, 1968), pp. 35-45. The quoted passages are on pp. 40 and 45. In this and the following quotations from this volume, I have occasionally modified the translation in the direction of a more literal rendering.

8"The Debate on the Critical Historical Method: Correspondence between Adolf von Harnack and Karl Barth," K. R. Crim, trans. in *The Beginnings of Dialectical Theology,* J. M. Robinson, ed. (Richmond: John Knox Press, 1968), p. 165/ *Die Christliche Welt,* 37 (1923), Column 7.

9 *The Beginnings of Dialectical Theology,* p. 167/ *Die Christliche Welt,* 37 (1923), Column 89.

10 *The Beginnings of Dialectical Theology,* p. 166/ *DieChristliche Welt,* 37 (1923), Column 7.

11 *The Beginnings of Dialectical Theology,* p. 168/ *Die Christliche Welt,* 37 (1923), Column 90.

12 *The Beginnings of Dialectical Theology,* pp. 37-38/ *Die Anfänge der dialektischen Theologie,* pp. 40-41.

13 Johannes Rathje, *Die Welt des freien Protestantismus: Ein Beitrag zur deutsch-evangelischen Geistesgeschichte dargestellt an Leben und Werk von Martin Rade* (Stuttgart: Ehrenfried Klotz, 1952), p. 463.

14 *Die Welt des freien Protestantismus,* p. 463.

15 *Die Welt des freien Protestantismus,* esp. pp. 84-95. For Rathje's more general reflections on shifts in the orientation of the *Christliche Welt* during this period, see pp. 100-114. For an extended plea that the *Christliche Welt* return to the position of the conservative Ritschlians like Kaftan and repudiate especially the radicalism of the religionsgeschichtliche Schule, see Gustav Ecke, *Unverrückbare Grenzsteine: Ein offenes Wort an Herrn D. Rade und seine Freunde* (Berlin: Landeskirchliche Vereinigung der Freunde der positiven Union, 1907). That Ecke had sympathetic listeners among the older Ritschlians is clear from Kattenbusch's remarks about the book some years later: "Unverrückbare Grenzsteine," *Christliche Welt,* 25 (1911), Columns 482-85.

16 See *Das Wesen der christlichen Religion* (Basel: Bahnmaier—C. Detloff, 1881), pp. 1-201 (all of the first part or division of the book). Kaftan's own characterization of this book in an autobiographical sketch takes considerable pride in his commitment to documenting his generalizations with references to the available data from the history of religions. See *Die Religionswissenschaft der Gegenwart in Selbstdarstellungen,* E. Stange, ed. (Leipzig: Felix Meiner, 1928), esp. p. 221.

17 That Herrmann self-consciously and systematically reduces the scope of what is considered the necessary historical base of Christianity is especially evident in his discussion of Ritschl's theology in his article "Christlich-protestantische Dogmatik" in the volume *Systematische christliche Religion* of the series *Die Kultur der Gegenwart,* P. Hinneberg, ed. (Berlin: B. G. Teubner, 1909), pp. 129-80. The discussion of Ritschl is on pp. 157-62. Herrmann rather sharply charges Ritschl with retreating to a new orthodoxy with its own set of revealed data because of his certainty that the Synoptic Gospels are reliable except for a few dubious passages.

18 For a particularly striking passage, see *Das Wesen der christlichen Religion,* pp. 74-76, in which Kaftan describes the heart of Christianity as "the hidden life of the soul with Christ in God."

In his autobiographical sketch, Kaftan draws particular attention to this mystical strain in his thought and to Ritschl's criticism of it. See *Die Religionswissenschaft . . . in Selbstdarstellungen,* pp 222-23.

[19]See *The Communion of the Christian with God,* J. S. Stanyon and R. W. Stewart, trans. (New York: G. P. Putnam's Sons, 1913), pp. 19-56. As a comparison of the first edition of 1886 with later editions indicates, Herrmann became increasingly explicit in differentating his position from others that might seem similar—in this instance, that of traditional, especially Roman Catholic, mysticism. Accordingly, my references are to one of the later (the fourth) German editions. *Der Verkehr des Christen mit Gott* (Stuttgart: J. G. Cotta'sche Buchhandlung Nachfolger, 1903), esp. pp. 16-46. The Stanyon-Stewart translation of 1913 was revised on the basis of the fourth German edition.

[20]*Das Wesen der christlichen Religion,* pp. 74-76 is also pertinent here. Kaftan argues that it is the very essence of religion to be consummated in union with God quite apart from any "Rückbeziehung" to the world—and that this is true of Christianity as well, despite its attempts to relate the religious and the ethical. See also his discussion of the kingdom of God as emphatically not equivalent to "the universal ethical community developing in the world" in *Die Wahrheit der christlichen Religion* (Basel: C. Detloff's Buchhandlung, 1888), pp. 547-55.

[21]*The Communion of the Christian with* God, pp. 202-356/*Der Verkehr des Christen mit Gott.* pp. 167-298.

[22]The references at this point could be indefinitely extended—an exercise that is unnecessary, since the contention is not to my knowledge a controversial one. Perhaps the agreement of Kaftan and Herrmann here despite all their differences elsewhere may represent the consensus. See especially: Kaftan, *Die Wahrheit der christlichen Religion,* pp. 547-55; Kaftan, *Dogmatik* (Tübingen: J. C. B. Mohr—Paul Siebeck, 1897), pp. 40-55; Herrmann, *The Communion of the Christian with God,* pp. 57-201/*Der Verkehr des Christen mit Gott,* pp. 47-166; and Herrmann, "Der Begriff der Offenbarung" in *Vorträge der theologischen Konferenz zu Giessen* (Giessen: J. Ricker'sche Buchhandlung, 1887), pp. 1-28. In speaking of a consensus, I do not mean to imply agreement in every detail. To take an example from the texts I refer to, on pp. 49-50 of his *Dogmatik,* Kaftan explicitly criticizes Herrmann for too narrowly focusing his conception of revelation on the inner life of Jesus. But despite such disagreements, both theologians see what they affirm as God's historical self-revelation in Christ as the distinctive and unparalleled center, ground, and norm of Christianity.

[23]Pfleiderer's entire theological program illustrates the efforts of liberals to resist Ritschlianism. The quoted phrases are excerpted from an 1891 article published in the *Jahrbücher für protestantische Theologie* and reprinted with two similarly critical essays (first published in 1889) as *Die Ritschl'sche Theologie kritisch beleuchtet* (Braunschweig: C. A. Schwetschke, 1891). The quoted phrases appear on p. 100.

[24]*Jesus' Proclamation of the Kingdom of God,* R. H. Hiers and D. L. Holland, eds. and trans. (Philadelphia: Fortress Press, 1971), p. 57/*Die Predigt Jesu vom Reiche Gottes* (Göttingen: Vandenhoeck & Ruprecht, 1892), p. 5.

[25]*Jesus' Proclamation . . . ,* p. 135/*Die Predigt Jesu . . . ,* pp. 66-67.

[26]*Jesus' Proclamation . . . ,* pp. 59-60/*Die Predigt Jesu . . . ,* p. 7. For a similarly forceful retrospective emphasis on this contrast between Jesus' own preaching and the needs of contemporary theology, see the foreword to the second greatly expanded edition of the book, *Die Predigt Jesu vom Reiche Gottes* (Göttingen: Vandenhoeck & Ruprecht, 1900), p. v.

[27] *Die Nachfolge Christi und die Predigt der Gegenwart* (Göttingen: Vandenhoeck & Ruprecht, 1895), pp. 130-47 and 151-56.

[28] *Die Idee des Reiches Gottes in der Theologie* (Giessen: J. Ricker'sche Verlagsbuchhandlung, 1901), pp. 110-55. See also Weiss's *Jesus von Nazareth—Mythos oder Geschichte* (Tubingen: J. C. B. Mohr—Paul Siebeck, 1910) in which he strongly criticizes Arthur Drews and others who purport to use historical-critical methods to reduce virtually all the Biblical accounts about Jesus to the status of myth.

[29] Gustav Ecke, *Die theologische Schule Albrecht Ritschls* (Berlin: Reuther & Reichard, 1897), esp. pp. 242-307. Ecke's attempt to distinguish systematically between Ritschl and these Ritschlians is remarkably parallel to Weiss's invocation of the authority of the master against the most prominent of his students. Ecke and Weiss agree that Ritschl is less traditional than his students—though they disagree in their evaluation of that difference.

[30] *Die theologische Schule Albrecht Ritschls*, pp. 119-27.

[31] *Christliche Welt*, 11 (1897), column 894.

[32] *Christliche Welt*, 12 (1898), esp. columns 76-81.

[33] *Christliche Welt*, 12 (1898), column 627. Compare Harnack's similar analysis in *Christliche Welt*, 11 (1897), column 894.

[34] *Christliche Welt*, 12 (1898), columns 627-31.

[35] "Erwiederung: (1) Die Methode; (2) der Supernaturalismus," *Zeitschrift für Theologie und Kirche*, 8 (1898), pp. 70-96, esp. pp. 70-73, 75, 82-83, 87, 91, 94-96.

[36] "Ueber historische und dogmatische Methode in der Theologie" in *Gesammelte Schriften II* (Tübingen: J. C. B. Mohr—Paul Siebeck, 1913), p. 730.

[37] *Gesammelte Schriften II*, p. 736.

[38] *Gesammelte Schriften II*, p. 736.

[39] *Gesammelte Schriften II*, p. 740.

[40] *Gesammelte Schriften II*, pp. 740-41.

[41] *Gesammelte Schriften II*, p. 743.

[42] *Gesammelte Schriften II*. p. 753.

[43] The 1892 version of Kähler's argument is a forty-seven page lecture. Accordingly, discussion of the views of others is very limited in comparison with the greatly expanded second edition. Most of Kähler's concluding chapter in this second edition is devoted to a critical comparison of his position with that of Herrmann. See *Der sogenannte historische Jesus und der geschichtliche Biblische Christus* (Leipzig: A. Deichert, 1896), pp. 155-206.

[44] "Der Streit über die Begründung des Glaubens auf den 'geschichtlichen' Jesus Christus," *Zeitschrift für Theologie und Kirche*, 7 (1897), p. 175; pp. 171-87 and 257-64 elaborate this cryptic

formulation. In an earlier essay, *Der Glaube an Jesus Christus und geschichtliche Erforschung seines Lebens* (Leipzig: Friedrich Wilhelm Grunow, 1893), Reischle does not employ this formalized distinction.

[45] *Zeitschrift für Theologie und Kirche*, 7 (1897), pp. 191-244.

[46] *Zeitschrift für Theologie und Kirche*, 7 (1897), pp. 244-59.

[47] *Geschichte und Historie in der Religionswissenschaft*, *Zeitschrift für Theologie und Kirche*, 21 (1911), zweites Ergänzungsheft, pp. 1-5, 22-24, 35-40, 46-47, and 72-86.

[48] *Geschichte und Historie . . .*, pp. 29-47, esp. pp. 40-41.

[49] *Die Christusmythe* (Jena: E. Diedrichs, 1909). An English translation was issued in short order: *The Christ Myth*, C. D. Burns, trans. (London: T. Fisher Unwin, 1910). For a helpful survey of the debate as reflected in both German and American literature, see B. A. Gerrish, "Jesus, Myth, and History: Troeltsch's Stand in the 'Christ-Myth' Debate," *Journal of Religion*, 55 (1975), pp. 13-35.

[50] Specifically with reference to his contribution to this series of exchanges, see *Die mit der Theologie verknüpfte Not der evangelischen Kirche und ihre Ueberwindung* (Tübingen: J. C. B. Mohr—Paul Siebeck, 1913), esp. pp. 31-44.

[51] *Die Bedeutung der Geschichtlichkeit Jesu für den Glauben* (Tübingen: J. C. B. Mohr-Paul Siebeck, 1911), esp. pp. 18-19, 23, 29-31.

[52] *Geschichte und Historie . . .*, pp. 70-71. "Invention" is Wobbermin's own word for the third alternative. Perhaps the use of the foreign term renders the oddity of the metaphor itself less obtrusive in the German text than in translation.

[53] *Geschichte und Historie . . .*, p. 82. In the following pages (pp. 82-86), Wobbermin examines the meaning and the implications of this flat assertion in some detail. He specifically considers the extremely hypothetical limiting case that Drews's most extravagant claims would be substantiated—that it would, in short, be conclusively demonstrated that a person like the one portrayed as Jesus in the New Testament accounts could not have existed in first-century Palestine. Even this eventuality, he contends, "in no way necessarily leads to the abandonment of the position of Christian faith." The reason he gives is the one that underlies his entire analysis: "The historicity—the historical availability—of Jesus is in no way the unavoidable presupposition of the truth of the New Testament picture of Jesus Christ" (p. 84). Wobbermin's glossing of "historicity" ("Historizität") as "historical availability" ("historische Fassbarkeit") is especially dubious in this specific context, since his discussion is explicitly about proof of Jesus' non-existence in first century Palestine. To justify the shift from the question of existence to that of availability (and thus to be consistent with his terminology throughout the essay), Wobbermin argues that historical research could never rule out the possibility that Jesus existed in some other time and place—and this possibility is all that faith would require (pp. 84-85).

[54] "Die Bedeutung der Geschichtlichkeit Jesu für den Glauben," *Zeitschrift für Theologie und Kirche*, 22 (1912), pp. 257-58.

[55] *Die Bedeutung . . .*, esp. pp. 10-17, 19-23.

[56] *Die Bedeutung . . .*, pp. 10-17, 19-23, esp. pp. 12-13, 15, 20. In a passing remark in another context, Herrmann refers to Troeltsch's analysis here. He maintains that Troeltsch's "stormy

eagerness" leads to overstatement, since he, Herrmann, is talking about Christian faith, not about people in general, and hence does not make negative judgments about non-Christians. See Herrmann, "Neu gestellte Aufgaben der evangelischen Theologie," *Zeitschrift für Theologie und Kirche,* 22 (1912), p. 77. In his critical response to Troeltsch, Fresenius makes the same point on Herrmann's behalf, along with his own affirmative statement about "other ways"; see *Zeitschrift für Theologie und Kirche,* 22(1912), pp. 250, 256-57. Troeltsch in his characteristic exuberance no doubt overstates his case. But his central contention remains: because of the continuing influence of conventions and assumptions from the established orthodoxy that they for the most part reject, Schleiermacher, Ritschl, and Herrmann do not explicitly and consistently execute the kind of historical or confessional and comparative theology that their underlying presuppositions would otherwise suggest.

[57]*Die Bedeutung . . . ,* p. 23.

[58]*Die Bedeutung . . . ,* pp. 23-25.

[59]*Die Bedeutung . . . ,* pp. 25-31, 40-51. For the contrast to Herrmann, compare esp. pp. 14 and 30. On pp. 45-46, Troeltsch emphasizes that he does not want to deny or belittle the importance that Schleiermacher, Ritschl, and Herrmann do attribute to the religious community. His contention is only that they do not consistently ground the significance of Jesus explicitly in the cultic needs of the church—and that the incipient moves that there are in this direction, as in Schleiermacher's *Speeches on Religion,* become lost in attempts to approximate the language of orthodoxy.

[60]*Die Bedeutung . . . ,* p. 32.

[61]*Die mit der Theologie verknüpfte Not . . . ,* pp. 20-21 is a summary formulation. But the entire booklet is intended to argue this point, as is indicated by the fact that the "distress" to which the title refers is said to be grounded in a reliance on externals rather than on the inner experience of faith.

[62]*Die mit der Theologie verknüpfte Not . . . ,* p. 44. See also pp. 27-32 for Herrmann's discussion of what he calls the "inextirpable possibility" that the figure of Jesus might be demonstrated to be the creation of religious imagination (Phantasie)—a threat which faith must struggle to turn into an occasion for joy in that it requires ever greater trust in God.

[63]*Die Bedeutung . . . ,* p. 32 for the quoted passages and pp. 31-35 for the broader discussion.

[64]*Journal of Religion,* 55 (1975), pp. 21, 30, 31.

[65]*Die Bedeutung . . . ,* esp. p. 40; see also pp. 4, 33, 37-38.

[66]*Journal of Religion,* 55 (1975), p. 31, esp. note 78. The references to Troeltsch are to *Die Bedeutung . . . ,* pp. 38-40, 43, 44, 50.

[67]"Aus der religiösen Bewegung der Gegenwart" (originally published in *Die neue Rundschau,* 1910), *Gesammelte Schriften II,* (Tübingen: J. C. B. Mohr—Paul Siebeck, 1913), pp. 40-41. The quoted passage concludes Troeltsch's discussion of "the latest sensation," namely that surrounding the publication of Drews's book. See pp. 36-41.

[68]*Die christliche Lehre von der Rechtfertigung und Versöhnung, Dritter Band, Die positive Entwicklung der Lehre* (Bonn: Adolph Marcus, 1874), p. 192.

[69]The third edition appeared in 1888; the quoted passage is on p. 214. The English translation is of this third edition, *The Christian Doctrine of Justification and Reconciliation: The Positive Development of the Doctrine*, H. R. Mackintosh and A. B. Macaulay, trans. (Edinburgh: T. & T. Clark, 1900), pp. 224-25. For an early analysis of the differences between the first and subsequent editions of Ritschl's book, see Friedrich Traub, "Ritschls Erkenntnistheorie," *Zeitschrift für Theologie und Kirche*, 4 (1894), pp. 91-129. See also Caius Fabricius, *Die Entwicklung in Albrecht Ritschls Theologie von 1874 bis 1889 nach den verschiedenen Auflagen seiner Hauptwerke dargestellt und beurteilt* (Tübingen: J. C. B. Mohr—Paul Siebeck, 1909). Kaftan, too, calls attention to the extent to which his *Das Wesen der christlichen Religion* influenced the later editions of Ritschl's work. See *Die Religionswissenschaft . . . in Selbstdarstellungen*, p. 223. A helpful recent comparative study of Ritschl and Herrmann is Hermann Timm, *Theorie und Praxis in der Theologie Albrecht Ritschls und Wilhelm Herrmanns* (Gütersloh: Gerd Mohn, 1967), esp. pp. 55-61 and 97-102, where he calls attention to this development in Ritschl's position.

[70]Herrmann's essay is entitled "Die Lage und Aufgabe der evangelischen Dogmatik in der Gegenwart" and originally appeared in the *Zeitschrift für Theologie und Kirche* in 1907. It is reprinted in his *Gesammelte Aufsätze*, F. W. Schmidt, ed. (Tübingen: J. C. B. Mohr—Paul Siebeck, 1923), pp. 95-188. The introductory reference to Troeltsch's article is on p. 95. The Troeltsch essay, "Protestantisches Christentum und Kirche in der Neuzeit," is available both in the first edition of 1906 and in the expanded second edition of *Kultur der Gegenwart*, P. Hinneberg, ed. (Berlin: B. G. Teubner, 1909), Teil I, Abteilung, IV.1, pp. 431-792. Edited excerpts from this article appear in *Gesammelte Schriften IV*, H. Baron, ed. (Tübigen: J. C. B. Mohr—Paul Siebeck, 1925, pp. 156-66, 191-202; see the editorial note on p. x.

[71]*Gesammelte Aufsätze*, esp. pp. 95-102.

[72]*Gesammelte Aufsätze*, pp. 98, 100-101, 128-33, 137, 139.

[73]*Gesammelte Aufsätze*, pp. 102-19.

[74]*Gesammelte Aufsätze*, pp. 118-19. Troeltsch concurs in this judgment and speaks of Ritschl and his school as "the only legitimate heir to Luther." See the *Kultur der Gegenwart* article, p. 730.

[75]*Gesammelte Aufsätze*, pp. 142-43.

[76]*Gesammelte Aufsätze*, p. 170. In the text, this sentence is printed in spread type for emphasis.

[77]*Gesammelte Aufsätze*, p. 181.

[78]*Gesammelte Aufsätze*, pp. 148-49.

[79]*Gesammelte Aufsätze*, p. 153.

[80]"Rückblick auf ein halbes Jahrhundert der theologischen Wissenschaft" in *Gesammelte Schriften II* (Tübingen: J. C. B. Mohr—Paul Siebeck, 1913), p. 221. This essay first appeared in the *Zeitschrift für wissenschaftliche Theologie* in 1908.

[81]*Gesammelte Schriften II*. p. 223.

[82]*Gesammelte Schriften II*. p. 223.

[83]"Grundprobleme der Ethik, erörtert aus Anlass von Herrmanns Ethik," *Gesammelte*

Schriften II (Tübingen: J. C. B. Mohr—Paul Siebeck, 1913), pp. 570, 668. Troeltsch's extensive study was first published in the *Zeitschrift für Theologie und Kirche* in 1902—shortly after the appearance of Herrmann's Book.

[84]*Gesammelte Schriften II*, p. 627.

[85]*Gesammelte Schriften II*, p. 627.

[86]*Gesammelte Schriften II*, p. 627.

[87]*Gesammelte Schriften II*, pp. 606, 628.

[88]*Gesammelte Schriften II*, p. 669.

[89]*Gesammelte Schriften II*, p. 598.

[90]After providing an extensive exposition of Herrmann's analysis (*Gesammelte Schriften II*, pp. 552-616), the essay "Grundprobleme der Ethik . . ." develops this criticism in its multiple ramifications: with reference to Kantian formalism, pp. 616-25; in regard to the eschatological orientation of the earliest strains of Christianity and their subsequent development, pp. 626-53; and finally with specific attention to Herrman's harmonization of Christian ideals with the actualities of contemporary culture, pp. 653-72.

[91]See especially the section entitled "Der Dienst Gottes in der Kulturgesellschaft" of Herrmann's *Ethik*. It is pp. 191-213 of the fifth edition (Tübingen: J. C. B. Mohr—Paul Siebeck: 1913) with the quoted passage on p. 194. Substantially the same discussion, including the quoted sentence, also occurs in earlier editions.

[92]*Gesammelte Schriften II*, pp. 603-5.

[93]*Gesammelte Schriften II*, esp. pp. 654-58.

[94]*The Social Teachings of the Christian Churches*, O. Wyon, trans. (New York: Harper & Brothers—Torchbooks, 1960), vol. 1, p. 53/ *Die Soziallehren der christlichen Kirchen und Gruppen, Gesammelte Schriften I* (Tübingen: J. C. B. Mohr—Paul Siebeck, 1912), p. 36. Troeltsch draws the same contrast in "Grundprobleme der Ethik . . . ," *Gesammelte Schriften II*, pp. 634-35.

[95]"Was heisst 'Wesen des Christentums'?" as reprinted in somewhat revised and expanded form in *Gesammelte Schriften II* (Tübingen: J. C. B. Mohr—Paul Siebeck, 1913), p. 387. Compare Troeltsch's comment in the "Rückblick . . ." article of 1908: "With Harnack, Biblicism is constantly on the verge of passing over into pure history of religions" (*Gesammelte Schriften II*, p. 209).

[96]*Gesammelte Schriften II*, pp. 391-401.

[97]*Gesammelte Schriften II*, pp. 406-7.

[98]*Gesammelte Schriften II*, pp. 407-11 and 423-51.

[99]*What is Christianity*, T. B. Saunders, trans. (New York: Harper & Row—Torchbooks, 1957), esp. pp. 10-11, 18/ *Das Wesen des Christentums* (Leipzig: J. C. Hinrichs, 1900) esp. pp. 7, 11-12.

[100]*Gesammelte Schriften II,* esp. pp. 413-18. See also "Grundprobleme der Ethik . . . ," *Gesammelte Schriften II,* pp. 637-39 for a similar line of argument.

[101]*Gesammelte Schriften II,* pp. 420-23.

[102]"Das Urchristentum und die soziale Fragen." *Preussische Jahrbücher,* 131 (1908/first quarter), esp. pp. 454-57.

[103]*Gesammelte Schriften II,* p. 626.

[104]Both Troeltsch's description of Jesus' preaching and his concluding remarks emphasize the discontinuties between the first and the twentieth centuries. See *The Social Teachings . . . ,* vol. l, pp. 39-69 and vol. 2, pp. 991-1013 / *Gesammelte Schriften I,* pp. 15-58 and 965-86. The Similarity of Troeltsch's position to that of Weiss or Albert Schweitzer is striking. See: Weiss, *Jesus' Proclamation . . . ,* pp. 105-13, 131-36 / *Die Predigt Jesu . . .* (first edition), pp. 42-50, 63-67; Schweitzer, *The Quest of the Historical Jesus,* W. Montgomery, trans. (New York: MacMillan, 1948), pp. 328-401 / *Von Reimarus zu Wrede: Eine Geschichte der Leben-Jesu-Forschung* (Tubingen: J.C. B. Mohr—Paul Siebeck, 1906), pp. 327-401. For a concise and illuminating discussion of this complex of issues with particular reference to Troeltsch's 1910 essay "On the Possibility of a Liberal Christianity," see Walter F. Bense, "The Ethic of Jesus in the Liberal Christianity of Ernst Troeltsch," *The Unitarian Universalist Christian,* 29 / No. 1-2 (1974), pp. 16-26; Bense's translation of the essay on liberal Christianity appears in the same number on pp. 27-38 along with some selections from Troeltsch's "Grundprobleme der Ethik . . ." on pp. 38-45.

[105]"Festrede im Namen der Georg-Augusts-Universität zur Feier ihres 150. Jährigen Bestehen am 8. August 1887 gehalten" (Göttingen: Dieterichsche Universitäts-Buchdruckerei, 1887), pp. 10, 17-18.

[106]"Festrede . . . ," p. 15.

[107]"Festrede . . . ," pp. 15-16.

[108]"Festrede . . . ," pp. 17-18.

[109]"An die Geistlichen unserer evangelischen Landeskirche" in *Quellen zur Geschichte des deutschen Protestantismus (1871-1945),* K. Kupisch, ed. (Göttingen: Musterschmidt-Verlag, 1960), pp. 74-75.

[110]"Erlass des Evangelischen Oberkirchenrats über die Beteiligung der Pfarrer an der sozialpolitischen Bewegung" in *Quellen zur Geschichte des deutschen Protestantismus (1871-1945),* K. Kupisch, ed. (Göttingen: Musterschmidt-Verlag, 1960), p. 86.

[111]*Quellen . . . ,* p. 87.

[112]*Quellen . . . ,* p. 87.

[113]*Kulturprotestantismus und soziale Frage* (Tübingen: J. C. B. Mohr—Paul Siebeck, 1970), esp. pp. 95-116. For a discussion of this development with specific reference to Herrmann's thought, see Hermann Timm, *Theorie und Praxis in der Theologie Albrecht Ritschls und Wilhelm Herrmanns* (Gütersloh: Gerd Mohn, 1967), pp. 89-153.

[114]This lecture appeared in the transcripts of the Evangelisch-soziale Kongress and was also published in the fourth supplement to the *Zeitschrift für Theologie und Kirche* of 1891 (its initial

year). It is most readily available as republished in Herrmann's posthumously collected essays: "Religion und Sozialdemokratie" in *Gesammelte Aufsätze*, F. W. Schmidt, ed. (Tübingen: J. C. B. Mohr—Paul Siebeck, 1923), pp. 463-89, esp. pp. 464-66.

[115]*Gesammelte Aufsätze*, pp. 484-85.

[116]"Christentum und Wirtschaftsordnung" in *Bericht über die Verhandlungen des vierten Evangelisch-sozialen Kongresses* (Berlin: Rehtwisch & Langewort, 1893), p. 12 (for his statement of the summary theses, from which the quoted phrases are taken) and pp. 12-19 (for Kaftan's elaboration).

[117]*Bericht . . .* , p. 12 (for the summary theses) and pp. 23-24 (for the elaboration, from which the quoted phrases are taken).

[118]*Bericht . . .* , p. 12 (for the summary theses, from which the first quotation is taken) and pp. 31-32, 34 (for the elaboration, from which the other quoted phrases are taken).

[119]*Bericht . . .* , pp. 36-37. This response is also available in Naumann's *Werke I*, W. Uhsadel, ed (Köln: Westdeutscher Verlag, 1964), pp. 334-40.

[120]*Bericht . . .* , pp. 35-36, 38-39.

[121]*Bericht . . .* , pp. 41-42.

[122]*Friedrich Naumanns theologischer Widerruf* (München: Chr. Kaiser Verlag, 1967), esp. pp. 34-68.

[123]*Briefe über Religion in Werke I*, W. Uhsadel, ed. (Köln: Westdeutscher Verlag, 1964), pp. 579-80, 601-6, 623-26.

[124]"Debattrede" in *Werke I*, W. Uhsadel, ed. (Köln: Westdeutscher Verlag, 1964), p 826.

[125]Schick's reference is in *Kulturprotestantismus . . .* , the note on pp. 105-6 and again on p. 114. Troeltsch's remarks are in response to Martin Rade's fulsome commendation of Herrmann's lecture at the preceding year's meeting of the Kongress as the necessary complement to Troeltsch's position. Herrmann's lecture especially emphasizes the authentic self's unity of will. For Rade's comment and Troeltsch's response, see the discussion following his lecture, "Die christliche Ethik und die heutige Gesellschaft," in *Die Verhandlungen des fünfzehnten Evangelisch-sozialen Kongresses* (Göttingen: Vandenhoeck & Ruprecht, 1904), pp. 51-53, 56-57. Compare also Troeltsch's more detailed interpretation of Herrmann's lecture in the course of "Grundprobleme der Ethik . . . ," *Gesammelte Schriften II*, the long notes on pp. 590-91 and 666-67.

[126]The differences with Ritschl (except the first one) are perhaps most evident in Troeltsch's concluding remarks: see *Die Verhandlungen . . .* , pp. 53-57. The references to natural orders are in the address itself. See esp. pp. 29-35. Troeltsch's lecture (in slightly expanded form but without the summary theses and the discussion and concluding remarks) is also available separately as *Politische Ethik und Christentum* (Göttingen: Vandenhoeck & Ruprecht, 1904).

[127]*Die Verhandlungen . . .* , p. 12 (for the summary thesis) and pp. 32-35 (for the elaboration).

[128]*Die Verhandlungen . . .* , esp. the summary formulation on p. 32.

[129] *Die Verhandlungen . . . ,* pp. 12-13 (for the summary theses, from which the quoted passage is taken) and pp. 35-40 (for Troeltsch's elaboration).

[130] For summary accounts of Troeltsch's views and actions during the last years of the war and in its aftermath, see: Gottfried Mehnert, *Evangelische Kirche und Politik: 1917-1919* (Düsseldorf: Droste Verlag, 1959), pp. 61-62 and 151-64; Fritz K. Ringer, *The Decline of the German Mandarins: The German Academic Community, 1890-1933* (Cambridge: Harvard University Press, 1969), pp. 190-213, 341-51, 396-98; and Friedrich C. Sell, *Die Tragödie des deutschen Liberalismus* (Stuttgart: Deutsche Verlags-Anstalt, 1953), pp. 362-64. Also relevant are of course Troeltsch's own essays in political commentary and analysis which appeared from fall 1918 until fall 1922 in the periodical *Kunstwart* and were also collected and published separately as *Spektator Briefe,* H. Baron, ed. (Tübingen: J. C. B. Mohr—Paul Siebeck, 1924).

[131] *Gesammelte Schriften II,* p. 653 note.

[132] Gogarten republished six of his essays as *Illusionen: Eine Auseinandersetzung mit dem Kulturidealismus* (Jena: Eugen Diederichs, 1926). The quoted passage is from p. 17. All six of the essays initially appeared in 1923 and 1924, the first five in *Zwischen den Zeiten* and the sixth in *Der Leuchter.*

[133] *Illusionen . . . ,* p. 133. Compare p. 90 and all of pp. 101-27.

[134] *Illusionen . . . ,* pp. 116, 118, 122.

[135] *Illusionen . . . ,* pp. 87-88.

[136] *Illusionen . . . ,* p. 126. Compare pp. 144-45.

[137] "Die dogmatische Prinzipienlehre bei Wilhelm Herrmann," *Zwischen den Zeiten,* 3 (1925), pp. 265, 267-68.

[138] *Zwischen den Zeiten,* 3 (1925), pp. 265-70.

[139] *Zwischen den Zeiten,* 3 (1925), pp. 272-74.

[140] *Zwischen den Zeiten,* 3 (1925), p. 274.

[141] *Zwischen den Zeiten,* 3 (1925), p 275.

[142] *Zwischen den Zeiten,* 3 (1925), pp. 246-47.

[143] *Die Christliche Welt,* 37 (1923), columns 305-6.

[144] The most directly relevant historical development is, of course, the collapse of Neo-Orthodoxy as a coherently advocated theological position. On the systematic epistemological issue, Hegel's *Phenomenology of Mind* already cogently (and in my judgment incontrovertibly) argues against the position Barth advances at least in this early period. For an elaboration of this claim through exposition of Hegel's argument, see my *Christologies and Cultures: Toward a Typology of Religious Worldviews* (Atlantic Highlands, N.J.: Humanities Press, 1974), esp. pp. 95-104. For a formulation of the issues that is less directly dependent on Hegel, see the first chapter (especially subsections two and three) of my forthcoming book, *Beyond Existentialism and Zen: Religious Commitment in a Pluralistic World Culture.*